Southern Fried Sass

Southern Fried Sass

A Queen's Guide to Cooking, Decorating,
and Living Just a Little "Extra"

Ginger Minj

with Jenna Glatzer

ATRIA BOOKS

New York   London   Toronto   Sydney   New Delhi

ATRIA
B O O K S

An Imprint of Simon & Schuster, Inc.
1230 Avenue of the Americas
New York, NY 10020

First Atria Books hardcover edition November 2023

ATRIA B O O K S and colophon are trademarks of Simon & Schuster, Inc.

For information about special discounts for bulk purchases, please contact
Simon & Schuster Special Sales at 1-866-506-1949 or business@simonandschuster.com.

The Simon & Schuster Speakers Bureau can bring authors to your live event.
For more information or to book an event, contact the Simon & Schuster Speakers Bureau
at 1-866-248-3049 or visit our website at www.simonspeakers.com.

Interior design by Jason Snyder

Manufactured in China

1 3 5 7 9 10 8 6 4 2

Library of Congress Cataloging-in-Publication Data
Names: Minj, Ginger, 1984- author. | Glatzer, Jenna, author.
Title: Southern fried sass : A Queen's Guide to Cooking, Decorating, and Living Just a Little "Extra" /
by Ginger Minj with Jenna Glatzer.
Description: First Atria Books hardcover edition. | New York, NY : Atria Books, [2023] | Includes index.
Identifiers: LCCN 2022060477 (print) | LCCN 2022060478 (ebook) | ISBN
9781668005477 (hardcover) | ISBN 9781668005484 (ebook)
Subjects: LCSH: Cooking, American—Southern style. | Minj, Ginger, 1984- |
Entertainers—United States—Biography. | LCGFT: Cookbooks.
Classification: LCC TX715.2.S68 M557 2023 (print) | LCC TX715.2.S68
(ebook) | DDC 641.5975—dc23/eng/20230104
LC record available at https://lccn.loc.gov/2022060477
LC ebook record available at https://lccn.loc.gov/2022060478

ISBN 978-1-6680-0547-7
ISBN 978-1-6680-0548-4 (ebook)

This book, and all the love in it,
is dedicated to anyone who has ever felt different.

Contents

Introduction

I was performing a sold-out one-woman show when my granny's words rose up in my mind: "Whatever you're given, you take it and make it better."

That's what I'd done. I'd been a short, gay, fat cross-dresser from a small-town family with no money, and I'd become a success despite it all. I hope that's inspirational to everybody who has any trait society looks down on. You can have shit piled on your shoulders till you feel like Luisa from *Encanto* and still gussy up your own life.

It's what southerners do. I know that being proud of growing up in the South can be controversial all by itself; people make a lot of assumptions. And to be sure, the South has some baggage it still needs to deal with, maybe in a giant group therapy session with mint juleps at the Piggly Wiggly. We can follow that with a glamorous statue-smashing party. But for me, it's also full of beauty. The South represents the art of taking not much and turning it fabulous. We see possibilities in places others overlook.

Who I am comes mostly from a succession of southern women who taught me how to love myself and others, how to cook, throw parties, handle criticism, ask for what I'm worth, and get through hard times. I went from being a depressed kid who felt like he didn't fit in anywhere to performing all over the world for audiences who appreciate who I am and what I do. That wouldn't have happened without people like my granny, my Harley-riding chorus teacher, and Publix's own octogenarian hussy Miss Betty Jean.

What they gave me was an ability to create my own path and do the things I love. What I've found is that I get great joy from cooking and entertaining, and that I connect with friends best when we're around a table sharing a great meal and talking about our lives. Down-home southern cooking is my specialty, and I've found that it works like magic to heal broken hearts, celebrate special occasions, and improve any random Tuesday. Also Wednesdays. My cooking can even improve *Mondays*. I know! Give it a try and you might just think, "What is this, Friday?"

Cooking has helped me to connect with my people, and my people have helped me connect with the world.

I've earned my pearls of wisdom, and now I want to share them with you. I've been counted out so many times in my life for being outside the norm, and maybe you have, too. My goal is to use the platform I have to help other people learn those lessons I did about celebrating yourself and having a better time in this world. So this is me, standing before you with arms wide open, ready to give you a pearl necklace.

LEFT: *Granny and me in the kitchen, cooking up some trouble.*

BELOW: *Say what you will, but Granny would always rock a hat . . . any hat!*

1

How to Love Yourself, Southern-Style

Now, as I'm sure you understand, my life is absolutely perfect and nothing ever goes wrong. My path as a gilded southern drag queen has been smooth as a Botoxed forehead. But if something ever *did* go wrong (and it never does, I assure you), then there would be one question I'd ask myself: "What would Shirley Temple do?"

Oh, not *that* Shirley Temple. (I'm sure she was lovely. Did you know she was ambassador to Czechoslovakia?) Anyway, that was my grandmother's birth name. For real. Granny Shirley Temple Lucas. Well, I mean, the "granny" part was added later.

She looked more like Snow White than Shirley Temple, but who can predict these things when you're a baby? Granny was the first person to teach me that I was worthy of love, and it's a lesson I've had to relearn and purposefully hang on to all my life.

She was born in Mascotte, Florida, a place that still exists, but barely. It's basically just a long country road and a community center, which makes my hometown of Leesburg, Florida, look like a bustling metropolis. Granny Shirley had lots of brothers and sisters, and she married a man who, by all accounts, was kind of an asshole.

Aside from being abusive, he also had a live-in girlfriend who almost killed my mother with bad oysters when she was about ten years old. That was a sore spot. She still can't pass a Red Lobster without crying. But then my grandfather *did* die (not from oysters), and my granny said, "I've spent so much time catering to someone who treated me and my children like garbage, and I don't ever want to do that again." So she decided she was going to stay a single mom and figure out how to support her kids on her own—a rarity in the 1960s.

As I made my way through my own life, I often thought back to that: how Granny decided she was going to turn her abuse into a superpower. You only get one shot at life, and if you spend that entire shot trying to do everything everybody else wants you to do, you're going to get to the end and be real pissed off that you didn't enjoy any of it. It's like going on a vacation with a whole bunch of people and doing everything they want to do, and then when you think it's about to be your turn to decide what to do that day, it's raining and it's time to go home. That makes me madder than a wet hen.

Granny cleaned houses, worked as a school lunch lady, whatever she could find. She didn't have any education beyond the sixth grade, but she was one of the smartest people I knew. I think that was partly because she was self-conscious about her lack of education, so she made up for it by reading books and watching documentaries. That woman would read *everything*—including encyclopedias—and she cared very much about handwriting, so she perfected hers until it was the neatest I've ever seen.

She cared passionately about racism and that made her eschew some southern classics like *Gone with the Wind*, because she couldn't stand the way it glorified slavery.

When the man I'd call my grandfather came a-callin', she told him she was too busy raising her kids to want to date anyone. But he was a divorced single parent, too, and he said, "I have my kids this weekend. Why don't we all do something together?"

They went to the county fair and hit it off like it was meant to be—the kids all liked one another, and before you knew it my grandparents were together all the time and fixing to get married. She loved herself enough by then to recognize that this man was worth her time.

My grandpa's first marriage was unconventional. When he was a teenager, he worked with a glass installer who got killed on the job when a big piece of glass broke. My grandpa felt responsible for the man's widow and kids, so he married her and tried to take care of them himself; that was his way. He was always someone who wanted to provide for others. As he and his wife both got older, though, they decided to go their separate ways.

Granny and Grandpa
cuddled up in the meat
locker for some reason.

He was ten years younger than my grandmother, but they seemed like an even match. My grandpa had a respectable job at Miller's Construction Company, and my grandmother had a dream of opening a restaurant. Which made sense, because cooking was her love language. If you showed up on her front doorstep—I don't care if you were a neighbor just dropping off some misdelivered mail or a door-to-door salesman or whatever—she was going to ask you one question: "You eat yet?" And then it didn't really matter much what you said, because she was going to cook for you anyway.

She was going to tell you to come in, and then she was going to put something together from scratch. Not leftovers. Not some microwaved bullshit. Something she decided on just for you, because she worried that once you left her doorway you might starve to death. She believed people were like baby kittens who needed to be fed every three hours or they'd just fade away.

Same solution for any problems that came your way. If you came to her with weight on your heart, whether it was relationship trouble or a bad report card grade, chances were that she was going to pull you into the kitchen and ask you to help her cook something or feed you something she had just made.

"This corn bread just came out of the oven. It's good. Let's put some molasses on it and then it'll be delicious."

She was like a virtuous version of the Hansel and Gretel witch, ready to fatten you up. When I was little and she needed to coax me to eat (yes, there *was* a time I had to be convinced to eat—hush your mouth), she'd find ways to connect food to my interests. I loved *The Wizard of Oz* more than anything, which was perfect because my granny came into this world in 1939 and she always took pride in telling folks that two American treasures were born that year: herself and *The Wizard of Oz*. She loved that movie and, in turn, got me hooked on it. Did you know Shirley Temple was the first pick to star in it? She was under contract to another studio, though, and they couldn't work out a deal. Probably for the best, because my granny might have combusted with excitement if you combined her two favorite things.

When she made corn bread, she didn't call it corn bread . . . she called it Yellow Brick Road Corn Bread (page 16), and it was the lightest, fluffiest corn bread you could ever imagine. She would coat the top with homemade honey butter and we'd chow down while watching Dorothy and her friends try to reach their own personal happiness. And my granny got me to try broccoli by pointing out that it looked like the green Wicked Witch.

Cooking was never just about ingredients either. Cooking meant stories.

"You know, the first time I had this corn bread was when your great-grandma and I made it in a skillet. We didn't even have a working stove at that time. We had to go chop the wood and get a fire going and then put the skillet right on the fire."

Somewhere between the listening and the eating, she'd distract the feelings right out of you. She knew how to make everyone feel special, and she expressed her heart through stories that were meant to make you feel less alone and more connected, and her recipes. What she made was soul food, down-home cooking from the rural South. It's called that because it gets right to your soul. If you're feeling down, there's something in Granny's kitchen that can heal you.

When I think of the high points of my childhood, it's my granny's cooking that comes to mind time and again. Cooking and sharing food with people became my love language, too. Whenever I'm home, my house is open to our friends, and my husband, CeeJay, and I love hosting. One year, when CeeJay was working and I was on tour, my mother and sister made Christmas dinner for all our friends because that was our tradition—they fed people they barely knew because they knew it was important to us.

So that's what I'm going to share with you. Stories and recipes and the potentially good advice I've picked up along the way (look, no guarantees). Because maybe you need it, too.

A few years before I was born, my granny's dream came true and they did open up a soul food restaurant: the Red Barn BBQ. My grandpa worked the kitchen and Granny was in charge of the front, with my mom and her brothers and sisters working as the waitstaff and kitchen help. It was very popular locally—eventually they even opened a second location that my uncle Rooster ran—and we'd practice new recipes at home.

For me, it started as these things usually do with kids: She'd let me hold the hand mixer with her or lick the spatula. I graduated to cracking eggs, and when she saw that I could do that neatly, she decided I showed promise.

"Let me show you how to pack and measure the brown sugar," she'd say, and I'd pay close attention because I knew everything she showed me was important.

Singing on the Counter

The only thing we didn't practice was my grandpa's barbecue sauce, because he was protective of that recipe—he wouldn't tell anyone how he made it, even us family members! He was afraid someone would steal it and then it wouldn't be his special recipe anymore and the restaurant's wouldn't be as popular.

I spent the majority of the first eight or nine years of my life at the restaurant when I wasn't in school. While I was still in diapers and just starting to walk and talk, my grandpa would pop me up on top of the long counter to entertain people as they ate. It kept me out of the way and the customers loved it. I'd sing and dance and they'd tell me how precious I was. Because I friggin' was.

Now, in the beginning it was just silly baby stuff, but as I got older, I wanted to put on a *show*. Costumes, routines. My granny helped me to decorate a jeans jacket with a bunch of pins, and that was my Tina Turner jacket so I could sing "What's Love Got to Do with It" in proper style with the collar popped like in the music video. I was probably too big to still be acceptably standing on top of the counter by the end of my run, but

LEFT: *Me mean-mugging the camera for Miss Linda's class photo. I don't know the boy holding my hand, but I thank him for his support.*

RIGHT: *My sister wearing me like a training bra at Granny's house.*

as long as the customers kept applauding, no one was going to stop me from doing it. It was my moment in the sun. Probably would have still been doing it now if the restaurants were still open. Fuck, that was fun. Adults have to at least pretend they're drunk if they want to pop up on a counter and sing to strangers. Which I do recommend. Take your moment how you can get it.

All of us cousins (and there were a lot of us) tagged along at the restaurant. They weren't into the entertainment part like I was, though. Most of them joined in when they were little, but as they got older they retreated and just wanted to play games on their own.

When I wasn't performing, we hung out in the back room or in nooks and crannies around the restaurant. My cousin Jennifer, who was two years older than me, and my closest friend, helped me get into trouble. At the drive-through window, one of us would pretend to be the cashier while the other rode their bike up to the window and placed a fake order, which would stop up the flow of traffic. Sometimes my grandparents would give us a couple bucks for "helping" around the restaurant so we'd stop screwing around.

Even when we weren't in the restaurant, we were all together most of the time. I was the youngest of four siblings by a wide margin—my sister was ten years older and my brothers were eight and nine years older—so Jennifer was raised more like a sister to me. She and her mom came to live with my family for a while after her parents got divorced, and she was good at getting me into trouble there, too. She'd wake up at 2:00 a.m. and tell me, "I'm bored," or "I can't sleep," so I'd do what my granny taught me about problem-solving: I'd take my best cooking skills and turn on the oven and whip Jennifer up a whole meal. Half the time she wouldn't even eat it, and then my mom would wake up for work a few hours later and say, "Why on earth did you cook a three-course meal in the middle of the night? What the hell?"

But I was learning to be a proper southern lady. I was finding the things within myself that I could do well and that I could share with others.

The Big Sipper

On weekends, my parents would drop my siblings and me at my grandparents' house, where we'd find ten to twenty cousins on any given day. Their house wasn't very big either—it started as just a two-bedroom place, but my grandfather expanded it himself over the years to accommodate the growing family. Don't ask me how he did it, but he taught himself how to do everything: building the structure, the roof, the electric, all of it. Whatever he decided to do, he would figure it out.

He was a man of multitudes, which also meant that he was a hoarder. The thing with him was that wherever he went, he wanted to gather up memories. *Everywhere* he went. Roadside stands, stores, gift shops, restaurants—he'd buy up the most pointless things. A velvet Elvis painting, a sunbathing frog on a lily pad under a palm tree, a plastic goat that pooped plastic hay, the breast-shaped "The Big Sipper" coffee mug that he got at some truck stop in Iowa. This was his way of commemorating and storing his experiences, and he never wanted to let go of any of them, because then it was as if you were erasing his memories.

I became sentimental about memories like that, too, but I learned from the mess I saw. At his house, it was stored all over on shelves, plus it overflowed closets, the garage, the patio, and a whole shed. I didn't want rooms full of "stuff," even though it fascinated me as a kid. Especially the pooping goat. You would feed it that same hay it just pooped out in an endless cycle. I mean, nothing is better than poop-recycling goats to a six-year-old.

As an adult, I've become a curator, and that applies not only to my things but also to my digital life. It's easy to become a digital hoarder and post about every thought that pops into your mind and every picture you take, but you have to ask yourself, "When this shows up in my 'Remember this day' three years from now, am I going to be proud I posted fourteen pictures of my extracted wisdom tooth? Am I just adding to the digital noise?"

The positive, though, was that he saw value and beauty in everything. He could find a piece of rotting wood on the ground and we'd say, "Grandpa, put that down—it's probably full of termites," but he saw something he could repurpose into something cool. That's what I drew on in the *RuPaul's Drag Race* costume challenges—"Of *course* I can make a shower curtain into a ball gown. I saw my grandfather do it when I was four years old."

Grandpa's claim to fame was that his family had owned a portion of the lands where the 1941 film *Swamp Water* was filmed. He was very proud of the Okefenokee Swamp, to the point where he insisted on taking us up there every couple years. He'd fill a water bottle as we were riding on a rental boat.

"Look how clear this is!" he'd proclaim. "You could drink this water."

Then he'd make us take a swig and we'd all about vomit. Giant alligators were crapping ten feet away.

"It's the cleanest swamp anywhere and that's why *Swamp Water* wanted to use it for their movie."

He'd bring that water bottle home with him, because now that was a souvenir, too. Dirty gator water.

Finding the Balance

One of the other important things I learned from my grandparents is that you don't have to find a partner who's just like you, but if you're going to be in a good relationship you have to be okay with balancing each other out. Every single person on earth except me has flaws, so you have to find someone whose flaws are tolerable, or at least entertaining.

My grandpa was a softie, leaving Granny to be forced into the disciplinarian role. He was just an oversized kid himself and wanted everyone to have the maximum

MINIMALIST SOUVENIRS

When it comes to collecting memories, think small. I pick up a Christmas ornament wherever I go on tour, even when it's out of season and I have to drive out of my way to find one. Then I know that at least once a year I will have a reason to look at my souvenirs—to touch and admire them—and a way to store them and put them away when they're not in use.

They're not all beautiful. We bought one at a roadside stand in Wales just because neither CeeJay nor I nor anyone we were with could figure out what the hell it was. So I asked the store owner, and he said, "Oh, it's a sheep!" It looked nothing like a sheep, or anything that was ever supposed to be alive. But it makes us laugh every time we look at our not-a-sheep.

Once my collection grew bigger than my tree (I've toured a *lot* of cities), I began offering them as souvenirs to my guests. Anyone who comes to my house at Christmastime is invited to take home an ornament they like, so now it's a double souvenir.

My mother collects three things: husbands, Precious Moments statues (which are Beanie Babies that have gone to confession), and spoons. Not from places she's vacationed, just ones she's stolen from restaurants. And I know I could get her some fancy handmade jewelry from places I tour, but a refrigerator-magnet spoon with a picture of Pennsylvania's state bird on it is going to mean more to her. It's the ruffed grouse, by the way. That's an actual bird, not just a nickname for Prince Andrew.

Consider how you might start a collection for your memories in a way that doesn't take up too much space. Postcards that you keep in an album or display on a wall, small figurines, books, rocks that you paint with the name of the town, pens, spoons. One of my friends has mason jars on a shelf filled with beach sand and little mementos from each of her vacations. I don't get snobby about souvenirs either: I think each person collects in their own way, and if you feel like it'll mean more to you to travel to Ol' Man Joe by the bay to get a hand-forged decorative horseshoe, then that's cool. But a shot glass from the airport gift shop is fine, too, if that's going to give you a happy memory.

Don't let your stuff take over or you'll have nowhere to store the important things, like your life-sized Ginger Minj standee.

amount of fun possible. At least once a week he'd take us out for sweets: ice cream, candy, cookies. Then we'd come home with bags and bags of nonsense and my granny would have to say, "You can pick *one* thing," because who wanted a dozen sugared-up prepubescent menaces in their house?

My cousins would call Granny mean, which was not helped by the fact that she'd paddle us sometimes. Once literally with our paddleball toy—she cut off the string with the ball on it and then whupped our butts with the little paddle for jumping around on the bed. And if one of us got in trouble, then we all got whupped for it. But you know? Some of those kids needed the whupping.

I learned what I wanted in a relationship from my grandparents. They were opposites in many ways, but they were so in love. My grandpa was an eternal optimist full of harebrained schemes and inventions—he was always sure that he had found an idea that was going to make them millionaires, and he would "invest" their money recklessly. He had no fears about the future because he was positive we were all going to be rich thanks to his wise investments. Grandma was the responsible one always having to rein him in.

She'd go through their restaurant inventory and say, "We have enough pork for this week. Did you order more chicken?"

"I didn't just get chicken; I bought us a chicken *farm*!"

You could just about hear my granny taking deep breaths and counting to ten in her mind.

"I don't want to be *mad* at you because I know you think this is a good thing," she'd say in a measured tone. "But let me sit you down and show you why this is *not a good thing*."

His heart was in the right place, but he was always getting them into pickles that she'd have to get them out of. His philosophy was "Go big or go home" and hers was "Yeah, but we need a home to go to." If she resented it, though, it didn't show. They were kind to each other, and spoke kindly *about* each other, which I didn't get to see between my parents. So from my grandparents I got my ideal and from my parents I got my warning label.

Both of them contributed to helping me understand what a healthy relationship was when I finally found one.

Granny's Kitchen

It was a bone of contention among the cousins that Granny treated me differently. She'd take me grocery shopping with her and teach me how to shop—"You start on this end of the store and work your way over. These are the things you always need to keep in a pantry . . ."—and how to balance a checkbook. It wasn't until I was older that I realized she didn't do that for any of the other kids.

She'd keep me in the kitchen to cook with her and kick the other kids outside . . . but that's because she seemed to understand that I needed her more than they did. I needed some extra protecting. Granny understood who I was before I did.

She was a progressive in a family of conservatives. I wasn't allowed to be myself at home, but at Granny's house I could be exactly who I was. I had a trunk of clothes there for dress-up play, and she never gave me a hard time about how I walked or talked or what I wore. I don't know how her kids didn't pick up her values, but they didn't. One of the last times I saw my granny, she was yelling at my mom to turn off the television because Donald Trump was on it.

What I learned early on was that the world could be a mean place, and that grandmas were good people to have around. I wanted to learn to cook not only for myself but also to make my granny proud of her protégé. It's the same way a teacher can change a kid's outlook on themselves by saying, "You're a great artist!" or, "You're so good at reading." Granny made me believe I could cook.

The first thing I baked from scratch was an apple pie when I was about ten years old. I didn't even like apple pie, but I liked the challenge, and apple pie was the ultimate southern way to prove your baking talent.

A basket full of apples sat out on the counter, so I pulled out my granny's Betty Crocker red lattice-cover cookbook and walked around the kitchen with my stepstool finding all the ingredients. I peeled and cut the apples, rolled out the dough, did the latticework, cut out shapes for decoration, baked it, and glazed it. Then I just left it out on the counter.

"Where did this come from? You buy this at Publix?" my aunt asked my granny.

"I don't know where it came from!" she said.

Everyone was checking it out and asking, and finally, I said, "I made it."

No one believed me, though, until I talked them through the process of what I did and the recipe I followed. Then they sat down to eat it, and everyone was so impressed with me. It was the first time I can remember all the adults in my family being complimentary toward me, and it made me want to cook and bake more.

I was meant to be a master baker, but I was afraid of hairy knuckles.

It was still another couple years before Granny would teach me how to fry things in a skillet, because she didn't own a deep fryer and instead liked to drop things into bacon grease, which was dangerous. I once saw a towel catch on fire, and she got blisters on her face more than once from splattered grease. I remember the day she first let me drop dough into a hot-oiled skillet, though, and feeling like it was an *accomplishment*. A rite of passage as important as getting your driver's permit.

I learned more than cooking in Granny's house. She taught me about discipline and neatness and manners. She taught me about writing by handing me a legal pad while we were watching *The Wizard of Oz* and asking me to write down all my favorite parts. The Wicked Witch became my favorite character in part because hers was one of the few names I knew how to spell. My granny could teach without making you realize you were being taught, because she had such a way of connecting with people and figuring out exactly what they needed and how they needed it.

She gave me an example of feminine power, always put together with her hair and makeup and nails done and her flowy floral shirts. And she taught me about empathy.

Years later, I'd remember the way my granny looked out for me in that kitchen and I'd recognize it when someone else needed protecting. Needed solace in a world that was too full of boxes and expectations. Or maybe just needed some corn bread.

Granny's Make It Better Menu

My granny never did have much, so she became very resourceful. She'd take whatever ingredients she had on hand and make things work.

The main tenet of her philosophy was to make use of everything, and to figure out ways to pass it along better than you found it. In that kitchen, we perfected her biscuits, her pinto beans, her pulled pork. Always trying one more ingredient or one new cooking method to see if it could be improved. Her go-to meals weren't fancy, but they were *correct*.

•

Perfect Pulled Pork

•

Granny's Yellow Brick Road Corn Bread

•

Granny's Rice and Beans

•

Baby's First Apple Pie

Perfect Pulled Pork

5 SERVINGS (OR 10 IN SANDWICHES)

"Pulling your pork" can be taken many different ways, depending on where you're at and whose company you're in, but either way it's bound to be mouthwateringly satisfying if you really take your time with the prep work. If the old adage "good things come to those who wait" is true, genuine southern BBQ is about as good as you can get.

1 tablespoon brown sugar

1 tablespoon onion powder

1 tablespoon ground mustard

1 teaspoon salt

2 teaspoons black pepper

4 pounds pork shoulder
(you can use butt, but I prefer the shoulder)

½ cup apple cider vinegar

2 tablespoons minced garlic

¼ cup apple juice

¼ cup white wine

1. Combine the brown sugar, onion powder, ground mustard, salt, and pepper in a small bowl and mix well.

2. Prepare your pork by trimming the excess fat and cutting the pork into four equal chunks.

3. In a Dutch oven or deep baking dish, rub the dry mixture over your pork in a thick, even coat. Allow to refrigerate overnight.

4. Preheat your oven to 350°F.

5. In a medium bowl, whisk together your apple cider vinegar, garlic, apple juice, and wine until combined and pour around the base of your pork.

6. Put the lid on your pot (if you don't have a lid, tinfoil will work just fine!) and cook for 3½ hours. Remove the lid and continue cooking for an additional 1½ hours, basting the pork every half hour or so, until your pork is fork-tender and pulls apart with ease.

7. Allow the meat to rest for about 10 minutes, then use a fork to shred. A lot of people like to presauce their pulled pork, but I prefer giving my guests the option of adding as much or as little as they like.

Granny's Yellow Brick Road Corn Bread

∽ 6 SERVINGS ∾

FOR THE CORN BREAD

3 cups all-purpose flour

1 cup yellow cornmeal

½ tablespoon baking powder

½ tablespoon baking soda

½ cup granulated sugar

½ cup brown sugar

1 teaspoon iodized salt

2½ cups milk

3 large eggs

2½ sticks salted butter, at room temperature

½ cup honey

FOR THE TOPPING

Honey and butter (to taste)

1. Preheat the oven to 375°F. Grease a 12 x 9-inch pan generously.

2. Combine the flour, cornmeal, baking powder, baking soda, granulated sugar, brown sugar, and salt in a large mixing bowl.

3. Add the milk, slowly, stirring as you go. Beat in the eggs, one by one. Add the butter and honey. Mix until well combined.

4. Pour the batter into your pan. Bake for 30 minutes, or until a knife inserted in the center comes out clean.

5. Slather more honey and butter on top and enjoy!

Granny's Rice and Beans

∽ ABOUT 5 SERVINGS ∽

1-pound bag dried baby lima beans

Chunk of salt pork

1 cup chopped onions

Salt and pepper (to taste)

1 teaspoon granulated sugar

Pinch of baking soda (to cut acidity)

2 cups uncooked white rice

1. Dump the beans, pork, and onions into a large pot and cover in cold water about 1½ inches above the ingredients. Add salt and pepper to taste. Bring to a boil and add the sugar and baking soda. Stir constantly for about 5 minutes, then lower the heat and simmer for 2 hours, stirring occasionally. If the water level gets low, don't be afraid to add more!

2. Once the beans are done to your satisfaction, remove from the heat and allow to sit while you cook your rice. Follow the instructions on your rice package for basic cooking time. You can make rice in whichever way you prefer, but my granny always started by adding salt, pepper, 2 tablespoons butter, and a dash of Old Bay Seasoning to the pot. It gives the dish a little kick that enhances it without taking away from the beans.

Baby's First Apple Pie

⌒ 8 SERVINGS ⌒

FOR THE FILLING

¼ cup orange juice

1 teaspoon lemon juice

¼ cup water

1¼ cups brown sugar

6 large Red Delicious apples, peeled, cored, and sliced

2 sticks salted butter

2 tablespoons cinnamon

1 tablespoon nutmeg

1 tablespoon allspice

1½ tablespoons cornstarch

FOR THE CRUST

3 cups all-purpose flour

2 sticks salted butter, cubed

½ cup cold water

MAKE THE FILLING

1. In a large bowl, combine the orange juice, lemon juice, water, and brown sugar. Add the apples. Mix well or shake until the ingredients are incorporated and the apples are coated. Set in the refrigerator to marinate for at least 30 minutes.

2. Put the butter, cinnamon, nutmeg, allspice, and cornstarch in a large pot over medium heat. Allow to melt and mix together.

3. Add your apples to the pot and mix well to blend all the ingredients together.

4. Cover and allow to simmer over medium-low heat for 15 to 20 minutes, stirring occasionally to make sure nothing sticks or burns.

5. When the sauce thickens and the apples are tender (not mushy!), remove them from the heat and transfer to a bowl to cool.

MAKE THE CRUST

1. Put 2½ cups of the flour, finely sifted, in a medium mixing bowl and set in the freezer to chill while cubing the butter. Set aside the remaining ½ cup flour for dusting.

2. Add the butter to the chilled flour in the mixing bowl. Use a fork to incorporate it, making sure each cube is coated.

3. Incorporate your cold water a few tablespoons at a time, using the fork to work it into the mixture. Take your time! You don't want it to get too wet too fast.

4. Once all your ingredients have been mixed together, quickly work your dough into a ball, cover in plastic wrap, and place it in the fridge to chill overnight.

5. Preheat your oven to 425°F.

6. Using your leftover "dusting" flour, roll about two-thirds of your piecrust dough into a circle about 2 inches larger than your pie tin.

7. Lightly dust your pie tin and work your dough into it. Once it's firmly in place, use a kitchen knife or scissors to remove the excess dough and add it to your remaining ball.

8. Add your apple mixture on top of the crust, packing it tightly. You may have extra, depending on the depth and size of your pie tin.

9. Roll out the rest of your dough and place it on top of your apple mixture. Once again, use the kitchen knife or scissors to trim the excess dough. Use a fork to crimp and seal the edges all the way around your pie, then poke a few holes or cut a few slits in the middle to allow the pie to vent as it bakes.

10. Bake for 35 to 40 minutes, until golden brown. For a glossier finish, brush on a layer of melted butter in the last 5 minutes or so of baking.

11. Allow to cool and set for at least 2 hours before serving.

2

Living Southern Sass

For me, sass is the spice of life. It's the way you go from being a background character in the world to having a memorable part. Really, it's just about telling the truth in a funny way. Everybody loves sassy people, and when you're plus-size, people *expect* you to be sassy. (Sorry, skinny people . . . you're going to have to earn your sassiness. And have a muffin, would ya?) But Ginger Minj's sass machine fired up well before I ever donned a pair of heels. It all started in the fifth grade.

Let me tell you about the sassiest southern woman I've known. Her name was Sherry Dale, a fifth-grade teacher at my elementary school in Leesburg. Five feet tall and five feet wide, she was shaped like a bowling ball on toothpick legs, which made everyone wonder how she stood up at all. Some kind of anatomical engineering miracle.

She wore skintight shirts that were at least three sizes too small and she fringed them all on the sleeves and the bottoms. On the days she wasn't riding her Harley-Davidson (I have no idea how she got on), she drove this little Mazda Miata that actually tilted toward the driver's side. My mom and I always giggled when we drove behind her and her crooked car.

Sherry first noticed me when I was in kindergarten and performing in a little chorus show.

"You have stage presence," she told me in the hallway afterward. I had no idea what that meant—I was five, for crying out loud—but it sounded like a good thing. "I'm going to tell them I want you in my class in the fifth grade."

See, Sherry wasn't just a fifth-grade teacher but also the piano-playing bandleader and musical director of the local community theatre. So she was recruiting.

After that day, she would point at me every time she saw me in the hallways in school. "I want you in the fifth grade!" I don't know what made her so sure, but she remained convinced based on that one kindergarten show that I was meant to perform. "You come alive onstage," she said.

Sure enough, she convinced whomever she needed to convince that I should be assigned to her class. There is nothing surprising about that because everything Sherry wanted she got. She ran that school and she ran that theatre, no matter what her title said. There has never been a better example of the word "spitfire." Some people might call it a Napoleon complex, but I saw that woman go head-to-head with people well above her pay grade and I never saw her lose. She did not ask *questions*; she provided orders shaped like requests. Sherry struck fear into people's hearts.

There was never any money in the school budget for art or music. Everything went to football. But then Sherry would march into the office and tell them that we needed to put on a show and then suddenly we had a weeklong stint in the high school auditorium across the street with their band playing for us. She found funding no other teachers could get, and exceptions no one else was entitled to, because she willed it so with the force of her personality.

And a bit like with my granny, she had no problem showing favoritism toward me in class. One of our writing assignments was to write a letter about the Vietnam War, saying whether we'd choose to stay and fight in the war or run away to Canada. Everyone but me said they'd go to war.

"Well, that is just ree-diculous," she said. "You're going to fight for your country? Do you even remember what this war was about? Only one person in this class gave this assignment any thought at all, and he said he disagrees with the reasons for fighting and wants to keep his family safe and provide for them, so he's going to Canada, and that's the only person here with a brain on his shoulders!"

She didn't name me, but they knew who she must mean. It made me a target of scorn, but it also felt really good, like when I was dancing on the counters or when everyone liked my apple pie. *Huh. Maybe I'm good at writing.*

I was quiet in school, and within the family most of the time. I'd been yelled at and teased enough times by then to know that there was something about me that didn't fit in and wasn't acceptable, so I'd learned to mostly sit and listen and not talk much. But when Sherry encouraged my writing, it made me feel like maybe I had thoughts worth sharing. She had me write skits for the children's theatre program, and she had me help her write the script for the big Christmas show that year. Sherry might have been my first legitimate fan.

I liked using big words and detailed descriptions, not abbreviations and what we'd now call text-speak. It was my own version of dressing up my writing with matching makeup and purse and shoes—I took pride in what I wrote and wanted it to be polished. Plus, I got to channel my mental instability into writing all my inner voices into characters.

Sherry Dale's Devil's in the Details Eggs

12 SERVINGS

6 large hard-boiled eggs, cooled

2 strips thick-cut bacon

½ cup mayonnaise

2 tablespoons spicy mustard

1 tablespoon sweet relish

Dash of Tabasco sauce

Salt and black pepper (to taste)

Paprika

Dill (optional)

1. Peel and halve the eggs, setting aside the yolks for later. Cook the bacon to a crisp and set aside on paper towels to dry.

2. In a small bowl, mix together the egg yolks, mayonnaise, mustard, relish, Tabasco, salt, and pepper until smooth and creamy. Spoon the mixture into a piping bag and refrigerate for 10 minutes.

3. Chop the bacon into small shards. Powder the paprika over the egg halves. Pipe the filling into the cavities of the egg halves. Top with a few shards of bacon. Enjoy!

ell

"I want you to come to my theatre," Sherry told me. "You're gonna come work on a play."

I thought she meant that I would help to write the play, and I liked that idea. But she meant that she wanted me to be *in* the play, and I was far less sure about that.

elllle

Granny and me at the Melon Patch Theatre's annual awards banquet, showing off my Best Juvenile Actor award for Friedrich in The Sound of Music.

ollo

Sure, I'd loved singing and dancing on the counter a few years earlier, but that didn't mean I was actually *talented*, just cute. I had no idea if I could actually sing or act, and I knew that my father found me very embarrassing. I told her that I didn't think I could do it.

"I think I should just help you write," I said. "Not act."

"Listen to me. You're supposed to be onstage. I know what I'm talking about."

I wanted so much to believe her. I was forever putting on little plays with my friends and I had all kinds of big dreams about performing, but at the time I had terrible self-esteem and was pretty beaten down.

Sherry convinced my parents to let me take acting classes and ride to the theatre with her every day after school. Plus, I auditioned and received a scholarship, so my parents just saw it as free babysitting.

The Bay Street Players Young People's Theatre had two teachers and directors at the time: Deborah (pronounced "De-*bore*-uh") Carpenter (the taskmaster) and Sylvia Vic-chiullo (the cool mom who'd let you get into a little trouble here and there). Deborah was one of the founders of the program in the 1970s—the "grande dame" of the theatre—and never had any kids of her own, so she saw us as her kids. She was known for hitting the bottle a little too much, for being highly eccentric and energetic, and for wild acting talent.

Sometimes the more brilliant the performer, the more unstable and tortured they are underneath. She drank to quiet her mind, which was the same reason she loved the theatre—it took her outside herself. Every day when I left, she'd say, "Kisses on your

Deborah's Cast Party Ham

∽ UP TO 25 SERVINGS ∽

15 pound bone-in ham

Juice of 1 lemon

Juice of 1 orange

2 cups packed brown sugar

4 (20-ounce) cans pineapple rings in juice

Fancy toothpicks

1 jar (about 12 ounces) maraschino cherries (whole)

1 jar (about 1.25 ounces) cloves

1 teaspoon salt

1 teaspoon black pepper

1. Prepare your ham by scoring the surface in a diagonal crosshatch pattern (think of an italicized hashtag!) and pouring the lemon and orange juices over the entire thing. Take the brown sugar and pack it onto the ham by hand, being sure to get it into all the nooks and crannies of the score marks. Really get in there!

2. Now it's time to get artistic with it: cover the entire ham in fruit! Hold the pineapple rings in place with your fancy toothpicks, then place the cherries in the center of the rings, securing them with cloves right through the middle. Sprinkle salt and pepper over everything. Dump the remaining juices from the pineapple rings into the bottom of the roasting pan to absorb into the ham and to use for basting throughout the cooking process. Tent everything in tinfoil and refrigerate overnight.

3. The next day, preheat the oven to 350°F.

4. Leaving the tinfoil intact, pop the ham into the oven and allow to cook for about 4 hours (roughly 15 minutes per pound of meat), basting regularly. Remove the tinfoil for the final 20 minutes. Allow to rest, then slice and serve!

face, sweet boy," but she also didn't fake anything. If she was pissed off at you, you knew it. She once told me I was "as loyal as a whore" when I dropped out of her show to do another one I'd already committed to.

Her philosophy on much of the theatre world was "KISS," better known as "Keep It Simple, Stupid." When I was sixteen I wrote a version of *The Wizard of Oz* where I gave the Tin Man a girlfriend named Tinrietta and a whole love story line, and she had the unmitigated gall to make me take it out because it was "not canon" and "ridiculous" and "really fucking dumb." We'd scream at each other on the phone ("You're ruining my art! Tinrietta is a feminist icon!") but then never hold a grudge and all was well the next day.

Sylvia was her student who returned to teach in the eighties. After class, she'd pile a bunch of us into her Suburban and drive us to her beautiful home and cook us dinner while we watched old Broadway shows on VHS.

They both became surrogate moms to me.

The first performance I did with the Young People's Theatre was a Christmas skit for a tree-lighting ceremony, and I played an elf who was Santa's phone-answering service. I had two entire lines. As it came close to my turn to say my lines, I felt burning from my toes all the way up into my chest. Stage fright overtook me, and I worried so much that people were going to make fun of me. But I had promised Sherry and I was in costume, so I had to do it.

"You've reached Santa Claus, but he's too busy right now. Send us a fax, and he'll get back to you soon!" I shouted.

It was loud and overdramatic and people laughed. I remember looking over at Sherry and she was beaming.

"See? I told you you could do it," she said afterward. "So next time I tell you to do something, just do it and don't give me any flak about it."

That became an ongoing theme. She'd tell me to do something that seemed like too big a stretch—like going up an octave in a song—and I'd say, "I can't do that," and she'd say, "Yes, you can. Don't give me any flak."

Nearly every time, she was right. I could do so much more than I thought I could. The only thing standing in my way was me.

UNLEASHING YOUR INNER SASS

It's very easy to listen to the little voice in your head that tells you it's important to fit in, to go along, not to embarrass yourself or anyone else.

But that little voice is an asshat. If no one ever took the risk of embarrassment, imagine how boring the world would be. There'd be no music, no theatre, no art, no books, because every creative person would be too hamstrung by the fear of public criticism.

There were plenty of people who made fun of Sherry Dale. Sherry did not give one solitary shit.

"I earned my money to buy my Harley and I'm gonna ride it!"

Sherry also had a collection of wigs that were all fifties, sixties, and seventies styles, usually bright red, to cover up her thin white hair. She wore them all the time, and you'd be onstage seeing just this red wig bobbing up and down in the orchestra pit. Sherry never felt the need to make herself smaller or more camouflaged because of her body type or her age or anything else the outside world might have criticized. She had perfected the art of radical self-acceptance and she thought she was pretty awesome just as she was.

Early on in my time on *Drag Race*, I let other people pick costumes for me—I'd just give them money and say, "Oh, I have no idea. You decide." But I *did* have ideas; I was just afraid people wouldn't like them. Too risky. Once I let my fake hair down, I finally realized, "Oh, people are loving the fact that I'm here in twelve mismatched patterns and colors in a safari outfit," because it was unexpected and authentic and people can sense authenticity.

So the next time you catch yourself thinking, "Oh, those pants are so cute, but I couldn't wear *that*," or "I'm too old for a hairstyle like that," or "I wish I had the nerve to get up there and sing karaoke, but . . ." I need you to say, "Fuck it," and go for it. Even people who say they're wallflowers really wish they could stand out, and they can. Fashion and makeup and hair don't have age or body limits, and you're allowed to make a spectacle of yourself no matter how the world sees you. Take the risk. Find your inner Sherry Dale.

What Sherry did for me opened up new worlds. I became a theatre kid—it was the most important thing in my life, far more than math and history and (perish the thought) gym class. I was bored in school and not accepted at home, but at the theatre I could escape into these other characters and other worlds and be celebrated for my talent. But to get there took a willingness to fall on my face, because it was completely likely that the kids in my school were going to see me in my elf costume and make jokes about me.

Sherry is the one who hyped me up and got me to try it, and after that I was a lot more able to find my own motivation. I'd been so terrified, but once I'd said my two lines I was able to relax and have a lot more fun. That theatre became my second home and I made some lifelong friends there—mostly girls, but a few boys, too.

Sherry, Deborah, and Sylvia taught us to care about our characters' motivations, even if we just had two lines. We'd have to write out biographies of our characters with full backstories for Deborah's approval.

What was so wonderful about that time was that Sherry, Deborah, and Sylvia hyped me up in every possible way, so that I started seeing bigger possibilities for myself. I did really well in the acting program, but before long Deborah was also encouraging me to do costuming and to write and direct and produce. Probably just because I was free labor and never really left the theatre, but still.

So I started to think that maybe I could make my wildest dream come true: I could be Elizabeth Berkley in *Showgirls*.

Yes, I know *Showgirls* got a 22% on Rotten Tomatoes and won Worst Picture, Worst Director, Worst Actress, Worst Screenplay, Worst Original Song, and Worst Couple at the Golden Raspberry Awards—fuck, it even won *Worst Picture of the DECADE*. That is an *accomplishment*.

And yes, I know it was probably weird for an eleven-year-old boy to watch a movie with lines like "I got bigger tits than the fuckin' Virgin Mary," but I was positively *enchanted* by this movie. Obsessed.

It was the story of how a mousy little girl whom everyone made fun of ended up being the star of a big, glamorous musical production. She was a beautiful superstar to me. So I thought, "If I work very hard at this, maybe I can move to Las Vegas and be a showgirl, too."

I didn't know what drag was then, so it wasn't that I saw myself as a drag version of a showgirl. I just saw myself as a showgirl—the glamorous star. I turned out to be Henrietta Bazoom (Lin Tucci), whom I appreciate a lot more now than I did as a child. She's funny, she's truthful, she's the one who keeps the show going—and she's the only one doing her own thing, not trying to fit the mold.

It's this kind of energy that I encourage you to bring into all areas of your life, from how you look to how you interact with people to how you cook. Your cooking style doesn't have to be recipe perfect; it's allowed to be experimental and use unexpected elements. That's how I've found some of my best stuff, just by thinking, "I wonder if relish would work in this." Sometimes it does and sometimes it's just weird, but bringing sass into the kitchen is a great way to feel pride in what you create.

No-Bake Peanut Butter Bars

∽ 8 SERVINGS ∾

These delicious bites of peanut buttery goodness can be made with or without the chocolate layer, depending on how much work you want to put into them.

8-ounce bar semisweet chocolate (optional)

½ cake of baking wax (optional)

1½ cups creamy peanut butter

1½ cups powdered sugar

2 sticks unsalted butter, at room temperature

1½ teaspoons vanilla extract

1. Line a deep baking sheet with wax paper and set aside.

Optional: In a double boiler, melt the chocolate and the baking wax. Once it's smooth and shiny, pour the melted mixture directly onto the wax paper and let sit.

2. In a large bowl, mix together the peanut butter, powdered sugar, butter, and vanilla until smooth and velvety. Pour the mixture into the baking sheet, directly on top of the settling chocolate. Pat it firmly into shape and refrigerate for at least 1 hour.

3. Remove from the refrigerator, remove from the baking sheet by turning upside down, peel the wax paper from the top, slice into squares, and serve, chocolate side up. If you opt out of the chocolate layer, you can always sprinkle some extra powdered sugar on top to gussy it up a bit.

Through the years, I began getting cast in not only our children's theatre shows but also other community theatre shows and tours . . . things took off for me quickly, and my teachers said I was destined to be famous. That sounded all right to me. I did several shows with Mandy Moore, a young actress from Orlando. I also voice-acted books on tape and performed in a series of Christian movies for children—kids reenacting Bible stories. My claim to fame was playing Paul in *Blinded on the Road to Damascus*, where I got to be struck by a blinding light and then healed by Jesus and filled with the Holy Spirit.

When I graduated from the Bay Street Players program at age sixteen, they turned it over to me: I became the director for a couple years, and this is where I got most of my footing for my career. I refused to choose children's shows for the kids, and instead did full musicals like *Annie Get Your Gun* and *The Sound of Music*. They never said no to me—I'd say, "I want to do a production of *Hello, Dolly!*" and they'd say, "Okay, here's what we can give you," and I'd have to figure out how to make it work with the cast, crew, music, costuming, all of it. Making something from nothing. It was such a thrill.

I stayed in touch with all three of the women who got me started—Sherry, Deborah, and Sylvia—and they were so supportive when my career took off. Sherry passed away in 2014 and Deborah passed away in 2018, and I found out at her memorial service that Deborah had kept a scrapbook of all my media clippings.

"You're going to be my success story," she'd told me, and she was so proud when that came true.

I've learned that people aren't put into our lives by accident, and that we should take the risk of loving the people we meet. Sherry and I probably looked funny walking down the hall together, and she had some views that didn't match up well with mine—she was oddly conservative for a theatre person—but she saw me. She loved me. She opened up my world because I let her, and I think I opened up her world in later years, too.

You never know where your guides are going to come from. But when they show up at your door, let them in. You might have things to teach each other.

MAYBE YOU BELONG
ON A HARLEY

If Sherry had paid any attention to movies or ads on television, she'd know that Harley-Davidson was not advertising to her. They did not design with bodies like hers in mind, and the world did not expect a white-haired church lady teacher to show up riding one. But Sherry saw herself on one.

Even if you've gone your whole life being cautious and rule following, maybe it's time for you to have an adventure of self-discovery. I saw myself as a well-behaved kid. Right after I got my license, I was driving my friend David somewhere and we ran into road construction. "Slow down," he said. "I wanna get one of those traffic cones!"

"What?" I tried to lock the windows on him, but that motherfucker managed to reach out and grab an orange cone and hold it against the side of the car for about twenty seconds until a police officer came, siren blazing, and handcuffed us in front of the Taco Bell.

I was briefly terrified (I had no idea how much trouble one could or could not get into for being an unwilling accomplice to stealing a traffic cone)—but then everyone in town wanted to know the story, and it became bigger in the retelling. It didn't lead to a life of crime, but I did learn that it was exhilarating to take little chances that were outside what I expected of myself.

Sometimes you have to break the rules a little to find out more about what turns you on, whether that's trying motorcycles, podcasting, bird-watching, or being a small-time public nuisance.

3
Southern Resilience

Magnolias somehow became the symbol of southern women, which I think is bullshit because yeah, they're beautiful, but they bruise easily and they bloom for five minutes and if they get cold they faint dead away like one of those Elvis fangirls. Which is why I think daisies should be the symbol of the South, because they're the opposite of all that.

We couldn't afford fresh flowers or any of that kind of stuff growing up. We just had whatever my grandparents grew in their garden, which happened to be lots and lots of daisies. The traditional white ones with the yellow centers. They're super hardy—they grow in garbage conditions. And my grandfather would use those daisies everywhere: all over the restaurant, the house, and decorating the cake he would make every year for my granny's birthday. That's how they became my favorite.

Roses mean nothing to me. They're like diamonds—literally just rocks with status. We let the world tell us, "You've got to spend two hundred dollars on these roses or you don't really care," or "You've got to spend thousands of dollars on this engagement ring with the perfect diamond to show your love." For me, I'd much rather have things that are meaningful but didn't cost a lot. Instead of ordering two dozen roses, if you went and picked a couple daisies and put them in a mason jar and gave them to me, that means a lot more.

I think life gets so overwhelmingly busy that we let the world get away from us and we just try to spend an impressive amount of money to show our affection. As I've gotten more successful, I've gotten busier and time has gotten away from me sometimes. There are occasions when I've been tempted to throw money at a situation to make it easier to take care of. But then I realized I don't enjoy that as a gift giver. When it comes to Christmas and birthdays, I like to do my private investigating and drop little questions and try to figure out what's superspecial and important to the people I love, and then try to make that happen for them. I get just as much enjoyment out of it as they do.

Resilience on Display

Resilience is something to celebrate. You've made it through everything that life has thrown at you, and you're still out there doing your best. (Or maybe you're half-assing it; I don't really know, but I'm giving you the benefit of the doubt, okay?)

In my house, I like to keep items that remind me of my resilience in easy view. I have a whole wall of shelving that contains objects I've collected throughout my life that symbolize my journey . . . and the centerpiece is my ruby slippers.

The ruby slippers were an integral part of becoming who I am—who I've always been, really, but wasn't allowed to be in my childhood.

"Stop swishing!" my father used to yell.

I really didn't understand why he would say that to me—why he picked on me in ways he didn't pick on any other kids. When I was little, it seemed like whenever I was having fun he wanted to stop it. I'd be running around with the other kids doing exactly the same kinds of things they were doing, but for some reason, I was always doing it wrong. Too loud, too much, too swishy in the way I walked.

My father called me a cake boy, and I thought that meant he thought I was fat. I wasn't even offended by that, just confused. I'd really tried to understand what I was doing to make him so angry and so embarrassed by me. I didn't know that "cake boy" was nineties slang for "effeminate." Sir Mix-a-Lot even wrote a whole song about it. You can still find it on YouTube, though you probably shouldn't. It's a shitty song.

In church, my father glared at me and told me to keep my mouth shut. At other people's houses, he'd try to get me to sit still away from the other kids, like I was contagious with something. He was especially mean to me around the guys from the Quarter Midget Racing Association—he was the president of the club. Quarter midgets are tiny race-cars—they're one-quarter of the size of a regular midget racecar, and kids as young as five can race them. If they're crazy.

My father really wanted to get me interested in football, but the uniforms had absolutely no sequins. He also tried to get me into racing—it was his obsession—but I hated it. I crashed my car on the track when I was eight or nine, got out of it, and said to my father, "Do you want to make some money?"

"How?" he asked.

"Sell this car, because I'm never getting in it again."

He and my uncles would make a point through the years of telling me to "man up" or to "act like a man." That's what it would have been to me—acting. I was never "manly." I saw myself as a boy, but I also saw myself as a wife and a mother one day. I know that's bewildering, but that's how it was—when I played house with my next-door neighbor, I wanted to be the mother and she would get *so* bent out of shape:

"You can't be the mother! You're a boy! You have to be the father."

Did I, though? That's not who I felt like inside, and plus, in my experience, fathers sucked. Mine spent most of our time together yelling at me or criticizing me, and I found myself on the receiving end of his temper and disappointment frequently. I never knew when it was coming. No one around town would have believed that either; they thought he was the nicest guy. The quintessential "shirt off his back" kind. He was very, very likable and sweet, except to me and my mom.

He didn't normally come right out and use the word "fag," so it stood out to me when he finally did once. "Quit being such a fag." I can still hear it just the way he said it.

I tried so hard to be the boy my father wanted, but it wasn't in me. I wasn't ever going to be the military or sports type like he was. I wasn't going to be like the other boys around me in school. I wanted to fit in better and to make my father happy so he'd stop hating me so much, but how do you become someone you're not? I couldn't, and that made me an oddity in my little conservative southern Baptist town.

My mother wanted to stand up for me, but that wasn't much in her nature either. She was quiet, a well-mannered southern woman. Sometimes people would question her about me—hinting at the idea that I seemed too effeminate—and she would say, "He's just artistic."

Artistic? I couldn't draw for shit, and although I liked to put on little plays, no one would actually mistake me for an artist of any kind. But artists are allowed more leeway in the ways they express themselves. Who didn't love David Bowie, Prince, Grace Jones, Andy Warhol? If you could be entertaining, you were allowed to be different.

RELEASING THE JUDGMENT

I knew from an early age that I liked clothing that was traditionally women's and that I saw myself as effeminate and wanted to marry a man eventually, even if I didn't know what any of that meant in terms of gender and sexual identity.

All that was a secret, though, because of the lack of family support. I look now at kids like Lactatia, the pint-sized drag queen who was the flower girl at my wedding, and I imagine what life could have been like with a different set of circumstances. Lactatia was dressing in drag by age seven, with his parents' full support.

There are so many things we deny ourselves out of fear of other people's reactions. While I loved dressing up at Granny's house, I sure wouldn't have felt able to dress the way I wanted at school or church or anywhere else, and that carried through even long after I was no longer under my father's control. Ask yourself what you're holding back about yourself that you wish you could release, and then . . . release it!

It can be scary to do things that are outside what people have known about us. But the more we can do the things we want to, and be who we are publicly and not just privately, the more inner peace we can have and the more genuine our connections can be.

When it was just the two of us, I knew my mother accepted me. She's the one who bought me my very own pair of ruby slippers but made it clear that this was "our little secret" and that I wasn't to wear them in front of my father or my uncles.

Little secrets can be damaging, though. I loved those shoes, and I loved my mama for seeing me. But in the long run, what I learned from that was that the things I liked were shameful to others. And that meant *I* was shameful.

It took me so much of my lifetime to overcome that messaging.

Now I've learned to release that shame, and to celebrate the little boy who wanted to wear dresses and heels. I honor him in my home with those slippers on display, and I honor him by consciously congratulating myself on how far I've come. You have to think of yourself as a trusted friend; if your friends had dealt with the hurts you have in life, wouldn't you cheer them on and tell them how amazing they are for being upright right now?

I make it a point not to have secrets anymore. There was so much my mother wanted to sweep under the rug to keep up appearances, until that rug was a mountain we had to climb. You don't want that in your house. You want a clean house, no rug mountains. You can take the things you thought you had to hide and turn them into showpieces.

Getting Out of the Dark Places

Mental illness ran through my family, and I began having depression and suicidal thoughts very young. Combine my genetics with my life circumstances and it was probably inevitable. But I remember the first time I acted on these deeply unwanted thoughts was in the shower when I was just eleven years old, holding my dad's razor and thinking, "I could just end it now."

My childhood wasn't all bad, but it was stressful. We didn't have any money, so there was always that issue . . . my mother was never good with money, hers or anyone else's, which is probably why we never had any! My parents weren't responsible with finances; it was important in the South to keep up appearances, so my mom always had her nails and hair done and we had nice "status" clothes like my Tommy Hilfiger overalls—but we were constantly on the verge of real trouble.

And then there was the family dysfunction. The men in my family probably meant well—they thought they could "toughen me up" and that would prepare me better for adulthood, but it was really just abuse and bullying. No one needs to be abused to prepare them for future abuse.

My granny was my protector; she was the only one willing to shut the family down when they started ganging up on me. None of the men were willing to show affection to an effeminate young boy, so I went through family life constantly on the defensive. They'd gather around the table to pick on me together.

"Butch up, sissy boy," my uncle Rooster would say, and the rest of the men would join in.

"You think you're gonna get anywhere in life bein' all girly like that?"

"What you need is a good ass-whuppin', git you in shape."

She'd walk in and yell at everyone to leave me alone.

"That is enough of that! Rooster, shut your mouth and help me set this table."

She was so important to me, but I could not rely solely on her love to carry me through life. There were times it all felt like too much, like things were hopeless and that I was never going to have a happy life. I had compulsive thoughts about hurting myself, and I had to fight back hard against these thoughts, with the help of therapists and medication at times. That's another southernism I've bucked against as I've gotten older: the stigma about needing help.

Americans in general wrestle with this, but probably more so in small towns: you're expected to work through your problems privately yourself, not go to one of those "head doctors" or use medications. But therapists can help you see things more clearly, help you put your challenges in perspective and figure out your next moves. And medications can help fix your brain chemistry, which helps you to do the things you learn about in therapy.

Southerners are resilient people. Many of us have been through poverty, broken homes, loss of all kinds, and we keep finding a way to move forward. One of the most important lessons I had to learn was to care about myself more than I cared about anyone else's judgments of me. When you find yourself getting a little too wrapped up in how other people are seeing you, whether that's because you're a big ole whore who slept with the basketball team *and* the cheerleading squad, or whether that's because you don't have the "right" shoes or hair or car, you have to be able to stand in front of that mirror and say, "I'm good enough, and I'm smart enough, and gosh darn it, fuck 'em."

Walking Past the Block

Small-town life can be fantastic if you fit in. It can also be a nightmare if you don't. Leesburg was the kind of place many city people have never experienced except in movies. To give directions to my house sounded like this:

"Go around the two S curves and then we're the third dirt road on the right with the little wooden church on the end."

There were cow pastures and trees and very few streetlights, and most everybody worked at either the dairy farm or Cutrale, a company that produces oranges, orange juice, and orange by-products, kind of like Bubba Gump Shrimp. It was straight out of some clichéd old-timey movie about what people *think* the poor South is like. ("They didn't have clean water or many teeth, but they still had each other!")

My whole family lived on one big square block—Pioneer Trail—for a good portion of my childhood, and everyone worked at the family restaurant, so my worldview was extremely limited for the first half of my youth. There were so many cousins that we didn't socialize much with kids outside the family. We just walked down that one block from one house to the other.

But I remember the biggest breakthrough of my young life: when Jennifer and I were allowed to walk past the block.

I had always wondered what would happen if we kept walking straight at the intersection instead of turning the corner to the rest of the square, and now we were deemed old enough to find out. After that, we spent all our time walking around town, discovering things we'd never seen before. A church that had been converted to an apartment building, and a lake behind it if you kept walking. All kinds of things that felt very interesting to me.

Not sure if I recognized what a metaphor it was at the time, but I can tell you about it now—our lives became very much about exploring and about finding what was next, instead of continuingly just walking the same exact path we'd been doing for years.

When you don't narrow your view to the one path you've always taken, you can find so many things that catch your interest. That's part of what helped me to develop resilience; I began realizing then that my life didn't always have to be about the small group of people around me who were judging me harshly, and the small-town gossip, and the boxes I didn't fit into.

I didn't know what exactly was out there for me, but I was beginning to understand that I was not going to spend the rest of my life in Leesburg. There was a whole world out there, and if I kept walking I might just discover it.

Grandpa's Sausage, Biscuits, and Gravy

∽ 6 SERVINGS ∾

The one thing he made better than Grandma! It was the most comforting of all comfort foods and was his way of starting the day in a cozy space. I love biscuits and gravy for their own resilience; the gravy lasts a good long time, and you can put it on top of fried chicken or any other kind of meat, not just biscuits. If the biscuits start to go stale, you can make them into a strawberry shortcake.

FOR THE BISCUITS

2 cups all-purpose flour

2 teaspoons baking powder

½ teaspoon baking soda

1 teaspoon sugar

1 teaspoon salt

½ stick butter, melted

1 cup beer

FOR THE SAUSAGE AND GRAVY

1 pound sausage

Vegetable oil to coat bottom of the pan

1 stick butter

¼ cup flour

3 cups milk

½ teaspoon salt

1 tablespoon black pepper

½ teaspoon hot sauce of choice

MAKE THE BISCUITS

1. Preheat the oven to 400°F. Grease an 18 x 13-inch baking pan.

2. In a large mixing bowl, combine the flour, baking powder, baking soda, sugar, and salt loosely with a fork.

3. Mix in the melted butter and beer slowly, until combined into a lumpy, slightly sticky batter.

4. Drop the biscuits onto the pan and bake for 15 minutes, or until golden brown. Allow to cool.

MAKE THE SAUSAGE AND GRAVY

1. Precook your sausage in a large frying pan over medium heat with a little bit of oil (turn to make sure they're browned all around) and set aside.

2. In a large deep saucepan, melt the butter and flour over medium-high heat and allow it all to cook until it bubbles, then reduce the heat to low. Whisk to create a roux, allowing the flour to cook out for 5 to 6 minutes.

3. Add the sausage to the roux and slowly whisk in your milk, bringing the heat up to a boil.

4. Reduce the heat to medium-low and whisk in the salt, pepper, and hot sauce.

5. Continue to whisk over low heat for about 10 minutes as the sauce thickens.

6. Ladle generously over the biscuits and serve!

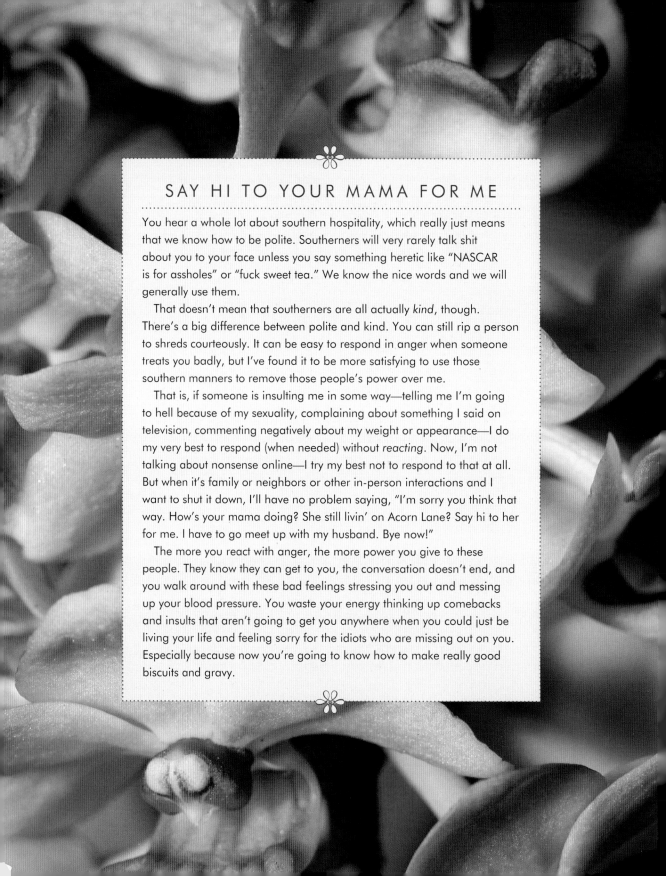

SAY HI TO YOUR MAMA FOR ME

You hear a whole lot about southern hospitality, which really just means that we know how to be polite. Southerners will very rarely talk shit about you to your face unless you say something heretic like "NASCAR is for assholes" or "fuck sweet tea." We know the nice words and we will generally use them.

That doesn't mean that southerners are all actually *kind*, though. There's a big difference between polite and kind. You can still rip a person to shreds courteously. It can be easy to respond in anger when someone treats you badly, but I've found it to be more satisfying to use those southern manners to remove those people's power over me.

That is, if someone is insulting me in some way—telling me I'm going to hell because of my sexuality, complaining about something I said on television, commenting negatively about my weight or appearance—I do my very best to respond (when needed) without *reacting*. Now, I'm not talking about nonsense online—I try my best not to respond to that at all. But when it's family or neighbors or other in-person interactions and I want to shut it down, I'll have no problem saying, "I'm sorry you think that way. How's your mama doing? She still livin' on Acorn Lane? Say hi to her for me. I have to go meet up with my husband. Bye now!"

The more you react with anger, the more power you give to these people. They know they can get to you, the conversation doesn't end, and you walk around with these bad feelings stressing you out and messing up your blood pressure. You waste your energy thinking up comebacks and insults that aren't going to get you anywhere when you could just be living your life and feeling sorry for the idiots who are missing out on you. Especially because now you're going to know how to make really good biscuits and gravy.

Saying Prayers

One of the things that centers me today is prayer, which I bring up with a big caveat: I've learned how traumatizing religion has been to many people, especially in the LGBTQIA+ community, and I'm not in any way promoting religion. That's your business, and I don't pretend to know any better than anyone else what's real and what isn't. I'm also specifically not advocating for the Christian church, which I think has gotten it wrong more often than right.

But I know that having a spiritual connection to a higher power has been a positive force in my life, and that doesn't have to mean the God of the Bible or the one I learned about in church growing up. It's *my* higher power, and I get to decide what that means to me, and so do you. I hope that everyone finds some kind of spiritual connection, because I think it can help you to feel more at peace and help you make decisions.

When I say my prayers at night, what I'm really doing is organizing my thoughts and speaking my intentions out there to the universe. I think there's real power in that. So here's what I do, in case this helps you, too:

* I say "thank you" for all my blessings, and there are lots of them. This gives me a chance to think them all through every night.

* I talk about the things I need.

* I talk about the things I may not need but still want.

This helps me to compartmentalize my life and figure out what's most important to me right now, and work through my issues one by one while also remembering how much I already have.

Prayer can function a lot like meditation or therapy, and the beauty of it is that you're never doing it wrong. It's your time to connect with yourself and the higher power you imagine, who always loves and wants the best for you. When I think about resilience, speaking my prayers out loud has been a big part of what's helped me to grow.

The other thing that's helped me grow is meat loaf.

Mama Minj's Meaty Loaf

∽ 7 SERVINGS ∾

My granny didn't fuss too much with red meat, but my mama loved the stuff! I don't know if it was an act of rebellion or maybe just a taste for the things she didn't really have growing up, but she tried to work beef into every meal. Her cooking was fine, sure, but it didn't have the soul my granny's food had. My mama cooked out of necessity, not because it was her passion. Except for meat loaf, which she made every Wednesday.

To this day, she still takes pride in her award-winning meat loaf. And I have to admit, it's a delicious mouthful of love! I never understood the "Oh no! Not meat loaf again!" complaints on TV commercials when I was growing up. Wednesday nights were solid. They were reliable. They were delicious! This meat loaf recipe has managed to bring even some of the most skeptical naysayers around to loving the dish.

A lot of meat loaves are the same texture and flavor all the way through, but hers is layered—every bite is a different flavor, and the texture is less bready than other meat loaves. It's less filler and more meat, and doesn't need to be dressed up with a lot of ketchup or gravy because it's already savory.

2 tablespoons butter

1 cup diced yellow onions

½ cup ketchup

½ cup molasses

1½ pounds ground beef

½ pound spicy Italian sausage

2 large eggs

2 tablespoons Italian seasoning blend

¾ cup Italian bread crumbs

½ tablespoon salt

1 tablespoon black pepper

½ cup chopped sun-dried tomatoes

1 cup shredded pepper jack cheese

1. Preheat the oven to 475°F. Grease your baking sheet or loaf pan.

2. Melt the butter over medium heat in a pan. Add the onions and cook until caramelized.

3. Mix the ketchup and molasses together in a small bowl and set aside.

4. Mix the ground beef, sausage, eggs, Italian seasoning, bread crumbs, salt, and pepper in a large mixing bowl. Please note, it's important not to overmix your meat or it will become tough! Just mix until it's all combined, not gummy.

5. Add the onions, sun-dried tomatoes, and cheese to your meat and give it a quick mix. Shape your meat mixture into a tight loaf. Make it pretty! Tent your loaf with tinfoil and bake for 30 minutes.

6. Remove the tinfoil tent. Pour the ketchup-molasses mixture on top of the meat loaf. Bake for 10 minutes more, or until the internal temperature reaches at least 165°F.

7. Let sit for 10 minutes to finish setting. Then stand back and watch them devour your loaf of love!

BOX UP YOUR THOUGHTS

CeeJay and I have done an exercise where we literally put our thoughts into boxes: We marked them "hopes," "fears," "wants," and "needs," and we wrote down our thoughts and put them into the boxes, then took turns reading them aloud. It was a great exercise for both of us that helped us get clarity on ourselves and each other so that we could be more supportive of our goals and wishes. Like sharing our prayers with each other. Give it a try!

4
Your People Are Out There

In my house, entertaining with love can look like everything from jalapeño strawberry jam to raspberry wig karaoke—and making sure everyone knows there's room to show up as their authentic selves.

I came out to my mom when I was fourteen, after a couple failed attempts. We were at the beach, staying in a two-bedroom time-share condo for a week with all my relatives, which was torture, and it came out in the midst of a breakdown. "I'm gay," I told her. "I don't know how to say it, and I don't know how to let you know that I'm not an embarrassment . . . I'm just gay."

"No, you're not. You're too young—this is a phase. It's just because you spend so much time around me and your grandma . . . you're just confused," she said.

That hurt, because I knew I was not confused. All my life I'd been attracted to boys. I hoped that she would be supportive, but in that moment she wasn't. Years later, I'd come to understand that it wasn't about her not accepting me, but about her not wanting my life to be any harder than it was. She thought she could talk me out of being gay and that would make my life easier. Not everyone understands that sexuality doesn't work like that.

I went back to being quiet about it, except among some of my theatre friends. None of them was gay, or at least no one was out, but it wasn't a big deal there. Still, I longed for someone to understand me. And then the craziest thing happened when I was sixteen: Our local biker bar was sold to two gay men, and they turned it into a gay bar. This was *scandalous*.

The local papers shouted out headlines like "The Homosexual Agenda Arrives in Lake County!"

All I knew was that I was going there. Somehow. I was dying to meet people like me . . . but I was five years away from the legal drinking age, and that was going to take *forever*. So I borrowed Jennifer's boyfriend's ID, and I waited until a costume night. No one would be able to tell the difference! Except . . . was I supposed to wear a ninja costume? A wizard left over from Halloween? My salvation came in the form of a themed night: Pimp and Ho. I was absolutely going to be a ho. A beautiful little underage ho.

The bar was called Attitude, and you had to park in a ditch across the street and run across the highway to get in, while rednecks stood nearby throwing rocks and bricks and garbage at you and informed you that you were going to hell. Satan himself had opened the bar to gather up more souls, you see.

I wore a wig and my sister's clothes and some borrowed makeup, and I looked like Carnie Wilson if she'd been on a bender where she'd already held on for three more days. It wasn't pretty, but the moment I walked through those doors I felt liberated.

Immediately, people were paying attention to me in a positive way I had never experienced. Boys wanted to buy me drinks and chat me up—"You're new here! Who are you? Where've you been?" There were drag queens who wanted to befriend me and fix my makeup—"I'm gonna be your mother. Let me show you what you're doing wrong and what you're doing right." I didn't drink alcohol; that wasn't the point of it for me at all. I just wanted to be somewhere I fit in for the first time. And I found it there, while drinking Coca-Colas and getting my eye shadow fixed.

DIVERSIFY YOUR CLOSET

Fashion, like gender, is nonbinary and nonconforming. You should be able to express yourself any way you feel, so make sure you have a closet that reflects your varying tastes. I have everything from tutus to tuxedos. Sometimes I go through romper phases. The more you feel like your look matches your personality, the more confident you can feel in attracting the right people into your life.

Only one queen at Attitude was local, and she ran an escort service. The others traveled in from other counties, sometimes long distances. It was the only gay bar around outside of Orlando, so it was something of a tourist attraction.

Nowadays it's so much more common for people to look for community online—we find social media groups or games or whatever with people who have the same kinds of interests and identities that we do and that's fine as a supplement, but it doesn't replace in-person interactions. It never will. You have to put yourself in situations where you will come face-to-face with people like you.

Without that little bar, I might have gone years more without ever encountering another openly queer person, and that would have been tragic, because it is *hard* going through your life feeling alone. Many of us have things that make us feel outcast or different, and it's important to figure out that you can be welcomed and loved for those same things that other people mocked.

After that first night at the bar, I wanted to be there all the time. I worked at Publix at the time, and I would put on my makeup in the break room at the end and get changed in the car before driving over. I got close with some of the queens there, so I eventually admitted my real age to them. No one ratted me out. They were protective of me, and knew I needed to be there.

On top of the rest of my challenges, my father had just walked out on us. His mother died on Christmas Day when I was fifteen, and his high school girlfriend showed up at the funeral . . . he left with her and never came back. That was beyond fine with me, but my mother fell apart. It hadn't been a good marriage, but it was twenty-three years of her life, and she wanted him back so badly that she tried getting me to call him and convince him to come home. "Tell him you miss him," she said. That backfired when I got on the phone and said, "I don't miss you. You don't need to come home. Things are much better without you here." For me at least. My mother hadn't figured it out yet.

"Is that really how you feel?" he asked.

"It's been how I've felt for a long time." My body was white-hot with anger, and I proceeded to run off a list of all the ways he'd hurt me, all the lousy things he'd done to make me feel worthless. After we hung up the phone, he didn't speak to me again for years, and that was okay with me. I was thrilled to be free of him so that my home could be a peaceful place.

My mother and I lived in an apartment for a while, where I was paying the bills. My mom had health troubles and I felt obligated to take care of her because she'd taken care of me up to that point.

But she was so lost that I recognized it wasn't healthy for me to stay with her any longer, so I moved in with her parents. I was rarely home between Publix, play rehearsals and directing the children's theatre, and the bar, and my grandparents didn't really notice the difference when I was coming and going in drag because they just assumed it was part of a theatrical costume. They were perfectly used to seeing me in all sorts of costumes.

They were very much "Whatever makes you happy" kinds of guardians, which was what I needed. They wanted me to have a job and to stay on a good path, but they didn't get worked up about my private life.

Even when my sister outed me to everyone.

Around the same time as I started going to the bar, I also learned about a magazine for gay teen and young adult men called *XY*. It was a quarterly magazine launched in 1996 with articles like "Where to Vacation Where Boys Can Kiss," "Prom Night," and "How to Pick Up a Marine." Lots of coming-out stories, nothing too erotic. I'd seen a copy at the bar, but they didn't have it in stores near me, of course, so I convinced a theatre friend to take me on an hour-long drive to Barnes & Noble in Orlando to get it. I had it in the bottom of my theatre bag, which my sister dug into one day. She showed it to the extended family while I was out running an errand at Walmart on Thanksgiving. I came home to a freaky tribunal assembled at my grandparents' dining room table. They were crying crocodile tears, passing the magazine around, launching into an intervention:

"You're ruining your whole life! You're going to destroy the family!"

"This is disgusting and immoral!"

That's when my granny walked in and grabbed me out of there. "Baby, come help me get the bread and let's put it on the table."

We delivered the warm bread and she said, "Y'all better start eatin' before the food gets cold."

WHERE TO MEET PEOPLE

There is somewhere for you to find community, and you should make it a priority to look until you find somewhere that feels like home each time you arrive. Here are some ideas:

CONVENTIONS: Comic Con, DragCon, Anime Expo . . . these big events are a lot of fun and part of the fun is just walking around and being entertained for the day or two, but the other part is about finding your people. Push yourself to actually talk to people, even if it's just "Where did you get those great shoes?" Don't be shy about making connections and asking to stay in touch.

FELLOWSHIPS: Church doesn't have to always be "churchy." Growing up, I was lucky to have a church that wasn't judgmental, but that can be hard to find. Some religions, like Unitarian Universalist, are known for being human focused and not doctrine focused. Look around and try visiting several fellowships to see if you feel comfortable at any of them—doesn't have to be the religion you grew up with.

DRAG SHOWS: Drag events are happening everywhere now—we've hit the mainstream. Yacht clubs and fancy-pants restaurants and everything. So if drag is an interest for you, get out and go to a drag brunch and meet people who are into what you're into.

Later that night, we were washing dishes together and she smiled and said, "I learned a long time ago that if you can shove their mouth full of love, they don't have time to spit out the hate."

Some of my family members softened up as they got older and some didn't, but my experience of family overall was not a positive thing. Some people get to have their own little tribe right there in their families, but that wasn't my experience, making it even more important to build your own family. Family's about who's there for you, not who you're related to through some genetic fluke.

Now, if it sounds like I'm encouraging people to do illegal things like sneak into a bar underage because you're too impatient to wait to find your community, yes, I am. I'm saying get a whole bunch of your high school friends together, wear pins that say "I'm queer," and wait for Governor DeSantis to come in ranting about groomers, Mickey Mouse, and how the KKK was too woke. (Dang, I hope my editor doesn't read this.)

What I'm really getting at is this: Human beings need other human beings. We don't need pictures on social media and text messages. We need touch and eye contact and gentle smacks on the shoulder and shared laughs and mischief. You need stories. You need to have that time when you and Gia and Ronnie and Luca accidentally stole someone's potbellied pig, because that's what will sustain you when you find yourself in a shitty situation someday. (Hopefully not in jail because you stole the pig.)

It's not just about individual friendships, but belonging to an entire group. There's a saying that it's not about quantity of friends but quality of friends, and *okay* and all, but you need *both*. Imagine your life with a posse. Imagine how it feels to walk into a room and know that you don't have to pretend to be anybody you're not, and you don't have to impress anyone, and no one's laughing at you behind your back unless you have toilet paper stuck to your shoe.

But you have to make that happen. No strangers are going to knock on your door to say, "Hey, I think we're meant to be friends." (Or if anyone is, that's really fucking creepy and you should close the door.) You have to actively seek out opportunities to meet your kinds of people and then actually follow through and take them instead of bailing because you feel lazy or socially awkward or you don't have anyone to go with or whatever.

Perfect Party Punch

⟶ 20 SERVINGS ⟵

8-ounce can crushed pineapple in juice

1 cup orange juice

2 tablespoons lime juice

1 bunch mint, chopped (leave out stems)

16-ounce carton strawberries, sliced

2 oranges, sliced

2 liters ginger ale, at room temperature

1 bottle sparkling Moscato

1. Mix the entire can of crushed pineapple, orange juice, lime juice, and mint in a large bowl, muddling the mint and mixing the juices until well blended. Freeze in ice cube trays.

2. Dump the cubes into a punch bowl and top with the strawberries and oranges.

3. Pour in the ginger ale and Moscato, helping to melt the flavor cubes.

4. Be sure to scoop fruit and flavor cubes into each glass as you serve, so every sip packs a punch!

NOTE: For a nonalcoholic version, replace the sparkling Moscato with 4 cups of lemon lime soda.

And then once you've met some people you like, you have to do what it takes to kick up those acquaintanceships into friendships. Invite people over. Do some shit with them. Yeah, it's risky and not everyone is going to turn out to be awesome, but it's worth getting burned sometimes in order to find the people who are going to wind up being your people.

My sister once invited a new coworker to come out with us to whirly ball, which is lacrosse in bumper cars. This woman was already drunk before we left. When she dropped the ball, she got out of her bumper car to retrieve it—and those floors are electrified! She got zapped good and fell upside down with her dress over her head and her panties hanging out on the floor, flopping around like she'd been hit with a Taser, before the ride operator shut it down.

"I'm fine! I'm good!" she yelled, and got back into her car, insisting they start it up again because she wanted to play. What's the harm in a little electrocution, anyway? Somehow we all wound up back in my apartment lighting sparklers in the dark and singing "I'm Proud to Be an American," which I have no memory of except that there's video. With an intro like that, there was absolutely nothing we had to hold back from this woman in the future. That's what happens sometimes when you take the risk and invite someone new along.

Maintaining Friendships

Now here's the other thing about finding your people: Once you find them, you have to keep them. That can take some effort. Some people are always waiting for the other person to make the calls, send the invitations, organize the plans. One thing I learned about friendship was not to keep score. You could spend your time getting irritated that you're the one who keeps reaching out, or you can just accept that Liza is distractible and forgetful, but you love her anyway and you call her whenever you think to.

I don't mean that you should waste your time with people who don't care about you. But I mean that as long as you feel love coming back from your friend, then go ahead and be the one to make the moves without worrying about who texted whom last, or who visited whom, or whatever. When someone's on your mind, let them know. Some people just get caught up in whatever's in front of them, but that doesn't mean they wouldn't be excited to hear from you.

The other important thing is to listen—really listen when a friend is talking to you. When things are exciting in your life, it can be easy to get caught up in talking about yourself and all the great stuff you're doing (or vice versa—when things are tough, you may need to lean on friends and get it all talked out), but remember that conversations have to go two ways, and that your friends will appreciate feeling heard and remembered. Ask what they have going on; ask what they're happy and sad about, their hopes and plans and worries. If they ask for advice, give it. If they don't, practice the fine art of shutting the fuck up about your opinions and just being encouraging, even if they're talking about dropping out of society and living in a grass hut and breeding screech owls.

Strawberry Pigs in a Blanket

∽ 20 PIGS IN A BLANKET ∽

**FOR THE PIGS
IN A BLANKET**

20 wooden skewers

20 mini smoked sausages

Vegetable oil (for frying)

**FOR THE STRAWBERRY
JALAPEÑO JAM**

2 cups crushed strawberries

1 cup minced jalapeños

⅛ cup lemon juice

¼ teaspoon black pepper

**¼ (1.75 ounce) package
powdered fruit pectin**

3 cups Splenda or sugar

**FOR THE STRAWBERRY
PANCAKES**

1 cup all-purpose flour

2 tablespoons brown sugar

2 teaspoons baking powder

1 teaspoon salt

1 large egg

1 cup 2% milk

2 tablespoons vegetable oil

2 tablespoons vanilla extract

**1 cup finely diced fresh
strawberries**

MAKE THE PIGS IN A BLANKET

1. Take 20 wooden skewers and pierce 20 mini smoked sausages all the way through. Set aside.

2. Heat a large pot of oil over medium heat.

MAKE THE STRAWBERRY JALAPEÑO JAM

Bring the crushed strawberries, jalapeños, lemon juice, pepper, and fruit pectin to a boil in a large saucepan. Once it begins to boil, slowly mix in the Splenda until dissolved. Return to a boil and allow to cook for 1 to 2 minutes. Remove from the heat and transfer to a serving dish or a mason jar. Serve warm or chilled.

MAKE THE STRAWBERRY PANCAKES

1. In a large mixing bowl, stir together the flour, brown sugar, baking powder, and salt.

2. Blend in the egg, milk, oil, and vanilla. Mix in the fresh strawberries.

3. Dip the skewered sausages into the batter, swirling off any excess. Place the battered sausages into the hot oil. When golden-brown, remove the sausages from the oil and place on paper towels to dry. Arrange the pigs in a blanket around the bowl of jam and serve.

"Yas, Queen. You go get those owls impregnated."

And if she later realizes that was a bad life plan, then you say, "Fuck those owls. Turning their heads around backwards is some creepy shit. Do you want a mimosa and a place to crash for a couple nights?"

I have tried to be there for my friends emotionally, physically, financially, all of it. Friendship should be about lifting each other up and being supportive of each other's paths, even when you're really damn sure they're screwing everything up, because how much of a market is there for screech owls, anyway?

Just know that there are people out there looking for you just in the same way you're looking for them. You're somebody's people.

EXPERIMENTING TILL YOU FIGURE OUT WHO YOU ARE

There are pieces of my identity that I knew for as long as I can remember, and other pieces that I was unsure about. If you're in a rut, it could be that you just haven't figured out some of the communities you're supposed to belong to.

When it comes to gender and sexuality, there's such an array of micro-labels now that might describe you—instead of just being asexual, you might be aegosexual (someone who has fantasies but doesn't want a sexual relationship IRL) or demisexual (someone who doesn't feel sexual attraction without an emotional bond first). Instead of being cis or trans, you might be a variation of nonbinary like genderfluid, genderqueer, or gendervoid. To get an idea of these micro-labels, try lgbta.fandom.com. If any sound right to you, there are Reddit groups devoted to many of them.

I used to think, "Okay, now we've gone too far," when I read about some of these more specific terms, but I've changed my view—I think it can be really helpful to dial into exactly how you feel and know that there are others who feel the same way. Weird like you. And it's okay to try on new labels and see if they feel right over time, because none of this stuff is fixed forever. Your sexuality and gender expression can evolve or bounce around, and you should always give yourself the space to discover new things about you.

5

Spike Your Sweet Tea with an Extra Shot of Joy

Southerners are big on adding a little extra sugar to everything. Mostly our food, but even some weird stuff. When anyone got a beesting, my granny would mix honey and sugar together and put it on, and when my face swelled up because I touched a hot pepper plant, she rubbed molasses all over it. Sugar really is the cure-all of the South.

They had a big backyard and my grandpa would get bored, so he'd plant all kinds of things just to see what would grow. He'd see some interesting plant on the side of the road and take a cutting and stick it in the ground and somehow it kept working. There was sugarcane there that we'd just chomp on, honeysuckle where you could suck out the nectar, and all sorts of sweet fruits, from watermelons to kumquats. It was like the redneck version of Willy Wonka's chocolate factory.

All that sugar, of course, is a metaphor for sweetening up your life experiences—making everything a little "extra," like any good southerner. In entertaining, as in life, I think we should all try to imagine how we can make every experience sweeter—to add some sugar and kick it up until it's flavored just the way we want it.

I learned how to "add my own sugar" as a young boy, and for me, that meant learning how to make myself happy on my own terms.

When you break it down, there's this idealized path that kids are expected to follow: You take your SATs, let your mama take five hundred pictures of you and your prom date in front of some trees, graduate from high school, go to college, get a job with benefits and a retirement plan, try to get promotions, join a gym, get married, have kids, retire, die. The yellow brick road.

I didn't just stray from the path. I blowtorched it.

I dropped out of school after the eighth grade. Not because I was struggling too hard for my grades—more the opposite. Even though I was dyslexic, I was still far ahead of most of the other students academically in my little town, so I was bored and unchallenged. But I could have dealt with that. What I couldn't deal with was the lack of any creative outlets and the way I felt more and more unwelcome socially. It wasn't a big deal when we were little kids, but as we got older there was more of a chasm between other boys and me, and I didn't have a place to fit in. I was tired of being bullied and picked on.

The high school had no drama program, no home economics department, no arts program to speak of. It was a small school dumbed down for these local kids, with a focus on athletes, and thinking about it filled me with dread because it didn't have anything left to offer me. There was no silver lining to my showing up every day. No sugar at all.

I don't think many kids get the option to think that through: "Will this help me? Will this serve me in any way?"

What I realized was that all it would do was ruin my mental health, with no benefit. In the performing arts, no one asks to see your high school transcript or gives a shit about whether you took AP physics. I wanted to better myself, and high school in Leesburg was not the path to that.

My grandmother inadvertently taught me that lesson. Even though she had very little formal schooling, she did value learning, and so did I. It's just that not all learning needs to take place in a standard classroom. There are many ways to get your education—both on paper and in the more genuine sense of the word.

I was already a working actor by then, and opportunities were coming up to tour regionally and to take jobs in Orlando and other cities outside Lake County that would require me to rehearse during the day. So I reasoned it through with my parents and grandmother and convinced them to let me homeschool until I could get my GED. They were not happy about it, but I was an independent kid and I wasn't going back to school.

I managed to cram all of high school into one year of a homeschooling program. This was the nineties, before remote schooling was even a possibility, so I had instruction by telephone, and then every couple months I had to go take tests, including all the standardized ones. I graduated at the end of what was supposed to be my ninth-grade year, and that was the end of my formal education.

You're probably expecting me to say: "Stay in school, kids," because that's what people do when they look back on their lives and realize they were too immature to make good decisions when they were teenagers. But no. I'd do it again, and I think it's totally possible that you or your kids should, too.

The normal accepted path is just not for everyone, and it's dumb for us to keep going on as if there's just one way to have a successful life. I think there are certain parameters that are important: You don't want to get lost in addictions, you want to be able to support yourself, you want to have good friendships and relationships, and you want to live somewhere that feels safe and right to you. If you can do that, I think every other part of how you get there is negotiable.

When I left school, despite my performing dreams I didn't necessarily believe they would come true. My life had been limited up to that point and it still felt like a far-off fantasy to think I could make a full-time living as an actor. I went to beauty school for a year, thinking I might become an esthetician, but skin care was the last part of the program and I couldn't afford to stay.

By my late teens, I had figured out that maybe Vegas wasn't ready for me to be a 5'4" showgirl, but I also knew I belonged somewhere bigger than Leesburg. So I started planning my escape.

Spiked Sweet Tea

∽ 1 GALLON ∾

Southerners are known 'round the world for their love of sweet tea. It may be a stereo-type, but it's certainly one we've earned honestly and wear like a badge of honor. Sweet tea is the perfect pick-me-up after a long day. Light, refreshing, energizing, and adapt-able! Sometimes you need your caffeine fix, but it's just too blazin' hot for coffee. Sweet tea is a drink that complements any meal, be it church picnic or fine dining. Simply put, sweet tea is nature's own little puddle of heaven!

But what only us true southerners know is that there are always two pitchers for every function. Observers usually assume one is sweet and the other is (pardon me while I gag) *un*sweet, but that's just not the case. One is your typical run-of-the-mill sweet tea, safe and fun for the whole family. The other is what my granny always called the Recipe. It was her cure for whatever ailed her. Heat, cold, energy, exhaustion, world hunger, whatever.

It was always in its own special dark blue pitcher (you know the one!) and was strictly off-limits to us kids. I didn't understand that she had added a "li'l something extra." It wasn't until I was older that I learned what Granny meant when she said she needed "a sip of the Recipe." One taste and I couldn't blame her—it's a crisp, cool drink with a slow, soft burn that warms you up and cools you off all at the same time.

People assume that we're all born with southern charm, but that's not true. Sometimes Jack Daniel's is our secret etiquette coach. Just be careful that your li'l something extra doesn't land you showing your panties on an electrified bumper car floor. Unless you're into that. Which is fine. I'm sure your panties are lovely. And so are you. Anyhoo, about that drink . . .

4 large tea bags

1 gallon water

4 cups ice

3 cups granulated sugar

1 cup bourbon

1 cup vodka

1 lemon, sliced into rings

1. Boil the tea bags in ½ gallon of water. Once the water reaches its boiling point, place a lid on the pot and remove from the heat to steep. Pour 4 cups of ice into your pitcher. Pour the sugar on top of the ice. Remove the tea bags and slowly mix the tea into the ice and sugar, melting them all together as you stir. Add the remaining ½ gallon of water until full.

2. Mix in the bourbon and vodka. Let chill for 30 minutes. Fill a glass half full with ice. Place a lemon ring on top of the ice in the tea. When the lemon ring reaches the top, you're ready to dive right in!

NOTE: Add a little less water for this version to make room for your alcohol!

Editing Your Life

What I think is that if you *could* be happier, then you *should* be happier.

It's simple, but I'm always amazed when people seem resigned to whatever they're doing even if they're miserable doing it. A friend will tell me they hate their boss and they're so sick of their job, but then they'll just keep showing up day after day because "it's a paycheck," with no plan to make a change. You know the type of job: the one where you have strict codes about what to wear and how many minutes you can take for a break, and how many holidays you have to work because they refuse to hire enough people, where they keep dangling the idea of a promotion or a real raise but never come through with anything beyond the bare minimum.

And yet when I ask why they don't quit, they say things like, "Where would I go?" or, "I don't want to start over somewhere else," or, "Oh, I'm just blowing off steam. It's a job." I think that's ludicrous. We all deserve to have jobs that don't make us depressed.

I regularly analyze my life to see which areas are working and which could be improved.

"Am I as happy as I could be with this?" I'll ask myself.

That could be lots of different categories: Am I happy with my work? My finances? My house, my community, my relationship, my free time, the way I'm taking care of myself, my travel schedule, my friendships, my achievements . . . I think taking stock of where you are and where you want to be can help you see more clearly about what can and should be changed. Don't get complacent—even if you think you're doing okay, is there room for improvement?

My grandpa was supposed to be retired when he wandered off to a tree farm up the road one day and came back with some news.

"Guess I'm not going to see you much anymore, 'cause I'm the manager of the tree farm now," he told my granny.

"What? You don't know anything about trees!" my granny said.

"We have trees right in the backyard! I kept 'em alive pretty good. It'll be fine."

Like many politicians, he never let a lack of knowledge hold him back. That man was not content sitting home in his retirement, so he went for a walk and changed his life—and he worked there as their star employee until we physically had to cart him away because his body wouldn't keep up anymore.

He understood the difference between keeping *occupied* and keeping *busy*. Busy burns you out. Occupied is when you're making time for the things you actually enjoy and things that will help you get to your goals.

I find it's also very important to make time for refocusing. CeeJay and I will often do a schedule of three months of heavy work and then one month off. During the month off, we have to guard against even talking about work, because it's very easy to get sucked into that—letting work and obligations crowd up your brain when you just want to be in your Hawaiian shirt sipping a blue slushie at Gatorland. At some point, you have to trust the foundation you've built and know that if you don't answer that phone call or if you put an autoresponder on your email saying you're on vacation it's going to be okay.

Life for me is about consistently making tweaks so that I can feel better and better about myself. I would not have been happy in a job with a lot of repetition and routine; even though it's a riskier path, I like the fact that I'm in charge of my own schedule (for the most part)—there's no boss telling me what I have to do or not do; I take jobs that

I want to take and I turn down the ones that feel wrong for me. It wasn't always exactly that simple; earlier on I had to take plenty of low-paying gigs that weren't the greatest for my self-esteem, but they were still in the field I wanted to be in. I knew that I was at least in the right orbit, even if it was going to take some doing to get from there to the kind of career I envisioned.

Nowadays I think it's easy to take advantage of YouTube and online classes to learn all about careers you might enjoy, and from there it's about having the guts to apply for jobs and seek out mentors who can get you going. You may have to start on a low rung, but you don't have to stay there long if you're vocal about your desire to move up and occasionally bring in some delicious baked goods.

Golden Tomato Quiche

∽ 6 SERVINGS ∽

Tomatoes are so taken for granted and so versatile. They're in every Italian dish in existence; they're in salads and sandwiches and soups. . . . I remember throwing a fit after my Wendy's spicy chicken sandwich was missing its tomato, because it ruined the whole thing—now it was too spicy, and not the right texture, and I felt I didn't get my money's worth because this very important part was missing. But that's what happens with staple foods and people—we overlook them until they're not there anymore.

Which is why tomato deserves to steal the show every once in a while. Behold, the golden tomato quiche.

2 tablespoons butter

1 cup finely chopped onions

2 golden tomatoes: 1 chopped, 1 sliced

3 large eggs

⅔ cup milk

¾ teaspoon salt

½ tablespoon black pepper

½ tablespoon dill weed

1½ cups shredded sharp cheddar cheese

1 unbaked pie shell

1. Preheat the oven to 350°F.

2. In a large skillet or pan, melt the butter over medium heat. Add the onions and chopped tomato and allow to cook for 5 minutes.

3. In a large bowl, beat together the eggs, milk, salt, pepper, dill, and 1 cup of the cheese.

4. Drain the tomato and onions and whisk them into the eggs. Pour the eggs into the unbaked pie shell and bake for 30 minutes.

5. Add the remaining ½ cup cheese and the sliced tomato to the top of the quiche and bake for an additional 20 minutes. Allow to cool and serve.

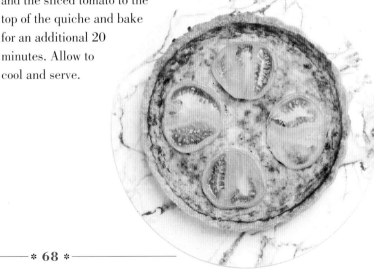

Moving Up on Purpose

My philosophy is that we all have the power to make big, positive changes in our lives if we're brave enough to do so.

There are lots of us who come from less than ideal circumstances, whether that's run-of-the-mill trauma like divorce or parental neglect or messes like poverty or abuse. The South has more than its share of generational poverty, which can stunt you because you have fewer opportunities, more dangerous neighborhoods, and this cycle where you can never really plan for tomorrow because you're always worried about just getting through today.

That can set you up for a lifetime of low expectations about what your future is supposed to hold. Sometimes you can get so caught up in just holding it together that you forget you're actually allowed to be happy. Does that seem like a frivolous goal to you?

We watch these documentaries about extreme religions where a woman is supposed to be okay with being the fifth wife and spending her life serving her husband and keeping her head down and not having any goals or dreams of her own, and we think, "How sad!" But so many of us are living less extreme versions of that. We're swimming with the stream our family set.

If they were rich, then we're likely to be, too. If they were poor, same thing. And if they were blue-collar, or married young, or Catholic, or whatever, then we get it in our heads that that's what's "normal." But who gives a shit about normal? We're not here to be normal. We're here to build something beautiful.

There were things about small-town life that I liked, and other things about it that felt wrong to me. But it wasn't easy to talk to my family about wanting to leave, because it felt like insulting their choices: If Leesburg was good enough for them, why was it not good enough for me? Most of my family still live there today, the kids doing the same jobs their parents did, making the same kinds of choices, dealing with the same financial crap.

But I could not make my life smaller to avoid hurting their feelings, and neither should you with your own family. There may come times when you realize that you have to throw in your cards and pick a new hand, or else you'll just stagnate where you are and never life the life that you know, deep down, you're meant to live. And that doesn't mean you have to know exactly where the path will lead you, but as long as you know you're not really happy, then you know you need to make changes.

Depending on your role in the family, too, there can be a lot of pressure on you to be responsible for others. Often the oldest child winds up in a babysitter-type role, and the youngest or middle child might be the one expected to stick around and care for aging parents. You might be expected to kick in toward family bills when you're a teenager, or to provide in other ways—like doing a lot of work around the house or driving siblings around.

The thing is, in some families nothing feels like a choice: Parents are authoritarian, and kids are expected to follow whatever they say. At some point, though, you need to break away from the weight of other people's expectations, because you're the one you get to live with. Just you. Everyone else is optional, but you're going to keep yourself company every day, and you have to like your own company. You can't do that if you're walking around sighing all the time about how you *could have done this* or *could have done that*, but instead you're the assistant manager at your dad's hardware store because you never spoke up and said, "No, thank you. I'm going to take a different path."

It wasn't just high school when I deviated from the path expected of me, of course. My whole career has been one long deviation from the norm. Some parts of it have been exciting and great and well paid, others have been one or two out of those three, and a few have been none of them. But I've stuck with the course until it paid off.

I don't mean I've never had a nonperforming job. I have—performing hasn't always been enough to get my bills paid, so I've been a receptionist, a barista, a costumer, a Tupperware saleswoman . . . we all do what we have to so that we can make it to the next step. And that's what life is—it's all just the next step and the next, with the ability to keep growing and doing new things.

When I talk about making changes in your life, I don't want to pretend that's always easy . . . if you don't have savings, a support system, other work experience, or whatnot, or there are things that make employers look down on you, then it can be challenging for sure. But find a way. You have to work toward that change, even if it's a lateral move and not something that's your "dream job" or ideal situation right now.

Sometimes when you're really down, it can be hard to see that next step, or even trust that there's one there for you. I had a young family member who was really spiraling into drugs and alcohol, who kept crashing the car and getting himself into trouble, and the change he needed was to move away and go into the military, where he has thrived. But he had to take that step instead of continuing to watch his life go nowhere.

I believe that all of us have places we're meant to be and things we're meant to do and if you don't get out there and check out the possibilities you could be missing out on something great. So don't do that. Do your thing.

Changing your vantage point can be everything. My sister had felt very stuck where she was, and I said to her, "You're standing on a dirt road and you're seeing only as far as the mailbox. I'm at a busy intersection and I'm looking at all these different paths all around me and I'm choosing the one that looks like it'll take me in the direction I want to move."

But you have to put yourself at that intersection. My best friend growing up, Adrian, was very much a pastor's kid. I somehow convinced her to run off to New York with me, which meant giving up everything—even her relationship with her father for a while. "If you go live this life of sin and debauchery, forget about coming home," he told her.

She wasn't trying to be an actress or anything like that. For her, the trip was about self-discovery: She knew she didn't want her mother's life, but she didn't know what she did want. Removing yourself from your environment can be eye-opening. And in the end, it's not that she became a trapeze artist and moved to Bali; she met her wife and moved back to Florida. The point isn't always to find your forever when you go on a journey; it's to figure out more about who you are.

It doesn't matter who you know. You can pick a spot on a map and just get yourself there and figure it out as you go. Adrian and I had garage sales and car washes and sold my car to raise the money for our trip. Whether it's a physical move or just a mental one, though, you can choose your direction and write yourself a new story line.

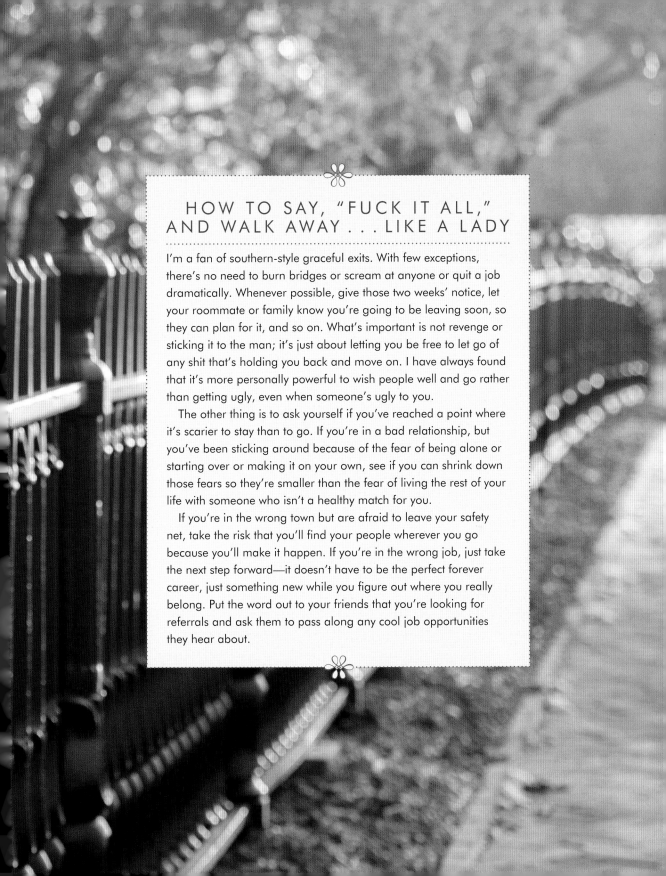

HOW TO SAY, "FUCK IT ALL," AND WALK AWAY . . . LIKE A LADY

I'm a fan of southern-style graceful exits. With few exceptions, there's no need to burn bridges or scream at anyone or quit a job dramatically. Whenever possible, give those two weeks' notice, let your roommate or family know you're going to be leaving soon, so they can plan for it, and so on. What's important is not revenge or sticking it to the man; it's just about letting you be free to let go of any shit that's holding you back and move on. I have always found that it's more personally powerful to wish people well and go rather than getting ugly, even when someone's ugly to you.

The other thing is to ask yourself if you've reached a point where it's scarier to stay than to go. If you're in a bad relationship, but you've been sticking around because of the fear of being alone or starting over or making it on your own, see if you can shrink down those fears so they're smaller than the fear of living the rest of your life with someone who isn't a healthy match for you.

If you're in the wrong town but are afraid to leave your safety net, take the risk that you'll find your people wherever you go because you'll make it happen. If you're in the wrong job, just take the next step forward—it doesn't have to be the perfect forever career, just something new while you figure out where you really belong. Put the word out to your friends that you're looking for referrals and ask them to pass along any cool job opportunities they hear about.

6
Holiday Magic

Southerners celebrate everything. Groundhog Day, Arbor Day, Sundays, you name it. We will find literally any excuse to decorate our houses, put on our fancy clothes, and bring a side dish in Tupperware to someone's house.

My philosophy on throwing a great party is that theme is everything. Head to toe, floor to ceiling, everything goes with the theme you choose.

Let's take Fourth of July. *Jaws* is the quintessential Fourth of July movie, and you're in luck: There are four of them, so you can play them in a loop in the background. What we did was hang a giant sheet by the pool and play from this cheap projector we got on Amazon while people were swimming. We got striped towels at Walmart for three dollars each that look like the ones in the movie, and everyone got their own towel. We made *Jaws*-themed snacks like shark cupcakes and trail mix in fishbowls, and served Bloody Marys—none of it has to be expensive, and it doesn't even have to be full meals.

You usually want to tell people the theme in advance (better yet, incorporate the theme into invitations) so they can dress the part. My best friend spends her whole year just waiting for her Halloween party to come around. She hand-makes all the decorations and people always say things like, "I can't imagine how much money you spent on all this!"

"I spent nothing," she'll tell you. "I went into the backyard and I cut down all the dead branches in the tree, I cut pieces of the bushes, I bundled them together, I spray-painted them and glittered them . . . I made this out of construction paper. . . ." You don't have to have a million dollars to be creative. The more money you have, the less creative you usually are.

But I swear to you, if you show up without a costume she will kick your ass out and make you go to Target and get whatever inflatable flamingo or giant foam pepperoni pizza they have left on the rack, because you do not show up to a Halloween party like some kind of non-costume-wearing fool, just like you do not show up to Christmas without something festive and preferably blinking in or around your face region. Have some fucking respect.

Oh, and hot tip: The rudest thing you can do is show up at a southerner's party on time. That's when the host is sticking on her clothes and spraying her hair and saying, "Shit! Everybody's about to be here!" But you also don't show up an hour late because that's rude, too. The correct time of arrival is fifteen to twenty minutes after what it says on the invitation. You will get put to work if you show up on time, guaranteed. "Oh, honey, I'm running so late. Can you make this punch? Can you go set these dishes over there? Can you go ahead and wrap fifteen sets of silverware for me?"

Now, the funny thing is that holidays weren't ever much good for me because my family didn't like me very much and I was usually getting yelled at or hiding from my father, and yet I still have really fond memories of the *idea* of these holidays—the parameters, the intent, the decorations and food and presents and excitement.

I know that's the case for a lot of families, particularly if you're LGBTQIA+—there's often a lot of family strife and bullshit that made the holidays unpleasant growing up, and that can leave you with emotional baggage that can make it feel like you're just getting *through* them rather than celebrating. Even in "good" families, holidays can feel like pressure and obligation. But that doesn't have to be your reality once you're on your own, because then it's up to you what to do with your holidays. And I say it's time to celebrate, because you're worth celebrating.

As I got older, I made my own holiday magic, taking the good pieces I learned from my granny and my mom and adding things I picked up or made up along the way.

Christmas, in particular, is a good month-and-a-half–long *production* in the South. Even before Thanksgiving, we were decorated and shining up the neighborhood until neighbors would come banging on the door at 2:00 a.m. asking us to turn off the lights because they couldn't sleep.

I learned that no matter how I was feeling, Christmas would always bring me a sense of peace and wonder. Lots of that is centered around the Christmas tree and its beautiful lights, so I put mine up early and leave it up late each year, and when I'm on the road I cart a two-foot miniature tree around to every hotel room and dressing room and set it up.

Each day, I use that as my meditation: Before anyone else wakes up, I get up and leave the living room lights off and sit by the tree with a cup of coffee and just let myself get lost in the twinkling lights and the beauty, with all my hand-picked ornaments and decorations. It helps me to wash away the worries and chill with myself, and then I feel like I can face the rest of my day.

Ahh, why didn't I start doing this right after Halloween?

I like the tree, too, because it's tangible art. If you're still just putting up the same tired box of ornaments you've always had because some relative got you a Bugs Bunny holding a candy cane and you don't have the heart to throw it out, but it doesn't really mean anything to you, stick it in a box and donate it. It's your freaking tree. Make it beautiful to you. I'm constantly tweaking mine to the point where my husband makes fun of me for it, but it's the same way I feel about my shows: I always want to make them a little better than the last one. So I move ribbons, I rebalance lights, I keep going until I feel like it's a masterpiece instead of just "good enough."

If it's a real tree, make sure you let it sit for a day for the branches to drop before you decorate. If it's artificial, invest in a good one—don't pick one you see that's already all dressed up on display, because a lot of those trees look like shit once you get them home. You need to see it naked, or at least read reviews of the model to know if it's going to look full and natural.

Start decorating from the inside out: Put your least favorite ornaments toward the inner parts of the tree to fill in the dead space, and your second least favorite ones toward the top because no one really sees the top. Your best ornaments sit closer to eye level. Then you tie it together with your bows and garlands and feathers or whatever makes you gag.

I'm usually on the road for the holidays, because holiday shows are so important to me. It's when I feel the happiest, and that gives me the right spirit for performing and sharing the joy. My first one was *Crossdresser for Christmas*, a spin on my one-woman show, but I found it was more fun sharing the stage. So since then, Gidget Galore and I pick different themes and tell stories and do vignettes between Christmas songs. We're not afraid to get stupid. Last year we did fifteen costume changes in ninety minutes. We did the story of *Frozen* in ten minutes, with Olaf on a puppet stick. We did a dueling banjos number where we came out and told awful cowgirl jokes like "Where does a cowgirl cook her meals?" "At home. Home on the range." "What do you call a cowgirl's outfit?" "Ranch dressing." The corniest shit, and people loved it. Over the holidays, you just want to let people turn off their brains and laugh.

~ooo~

Once I was an adult, I decided on an important rule for myself: I was no longer going to go to difficult family members' homes for holidays, but I was going to invite them to mine.

Why? Well, when you're the host, you get to set the moral tone and the rules. It's something I learned from my granny, because she had the ability to shut things down in her home. I recognized the power in that: "This is how it is in my house. You don't have to like it, but you have to be okay with it." That meant there were topics that were off-limits, and I sure didn't want to hear any homophobic judgment. Hosting put me in the power seat, so that my husband and I didn't have to spend my holidays feeling the way I did growing up.

When friends brought guests I hadn't met yet, I would greet them with something like this: "Hello! Welcome to my home. I'm so happy to have you here. In this house, we're having a party tonight, so leave your religion and politics at the door and let's have a good time." Take it into your hands and own it right at the beginning and give reminders if needed.

I think a good host will try to lead and steer conversations by bringing up positive subjects. When things get tense, you shut it down in a polite way by changing the subject. When someone really doesn't take a hint, you shove bread in their mouth.

Despite my "no religion" rule, I do have a little lamb made out of butter each Easter, and some wiseass will say, "We're not allowed to talk about religion, but you can have a butter lamb?" Yes, because it's decorative and adorable. Fuck you.

I didn't give up on my family—still haven't even though I know the odds of change are low—but I also didn't allow them to get to me. I had to build myself up to the point where I could be around them and not feel terrible about myself, and to be honest, some of that came into play after I started making a name for myself. I was able to see that I was becoming a success and most of them were stuck exactly where we'd been twenty years earlier, like a loop. So I practiced the fine southern art of Rising Above like a motherfucking plump little phoenix.

But of course, it's not just about family. My husband and I love to entertain our friends, and what we do most often is throw potluck dinners.

WHY TO THROW A POTLUCK

Aside from the fact that it takes the pressure off the host to do it all, potlucks are a great way to include everyone in the conversation, especially when not everyone knows one another well.

You invite a bunch of people who you think might be interesting together, and ask them to each make a dish that represents where they're from, or just something they love, and then it's a natural conversation starter: People wind up talking about their culture, their family, what they love, and how they came to learn the recipe.

Jiggly Caliente is such a fun person to have at parties because she's outgoing and lovable and an idiot who doesn't think before she shoots her mouth off. She got my mother to try Filipino food for the first time, which my mom was convinced she was going to hate. Jiggly brought these bright red sausage sliders and my mother was all "no thank you" until I talked her into it, and then her eyes lit up.

Most people *want* to bring something when you invite them to a dinner anyway, so it's better to figure it out in advance instead of telling people that you have it covered and then everyone bringing the same bakery cookies or eighteen bottles of wine. And speaking of wine, that's also a great saver for anyone who's not really a cook—you put them in charge of drinks or salad or bread.

Keep some disposable containers on hand so you can send people home with leftovers.

Food as Tradition

We were all really close on my mama's side of the family when I was growing up. Granny and Grandpa had eight kids between them, who, in turn, had twenty-one grandkids, which trickled down into forty-seven great-grandkids and eighteen great-great-grand-babies (so far!). That's a lot of folks, for sure, but no generation in our family grew up lonely. My daddy's side of the family was a different story. None of them spent much time together and there's still a bunch I'm sure I've never met. My paternal grand-mother was the glue that held that side of the family together and when she passed away they all seemed to go off in search of their own path.

Grandma Eads was an incredible woman. Loving, stern, and ridiculously intuitive. If Granny Shirley was Thelma Harper from *Mama's Family*, Grandma Eads was Edith from *All in the Family*. On the last Sunday of every month, we would make the two-hour trek to my dad's parents' double-wide in Lakeland for Grandma Eads' famous Sunday Supper. It was always exactly the same: French-cut green beans fresh from the can, slow-cooked pot roast, creamed corn, and the most delicious mashed potatoes in the world.

It's been almost twenty years since she passed away, and I can still taste those per-fectly balanced spuds. It took a decade to track down someone from my dad's side of the family who had Grandma's recipe, but I got it! And it's just as delicious as I remember.

Grandma 'Eads' Super Sunday Spuds

～ 10 SERVINGS ～

2 tablespoons minced garlic

2 tablespoons black pepper

5 tablespoons iodized salt

Handful of fresh dill

1½ sticks salted butter

5 large russet potatoes

1½ pounds baby Dutch potatoes

½ cup buttermilk

8-ounce container sour cream

Parsley leaves (for garnish)

1. Put a pot of water on to boil. Season the water with 1 tablespoon of the garlic, 1 tablespoon of the pepper, 2½ tablespoons of the salt, and the dill.

2. Slice the ½ stick of the butter into ⅛-inch chips and chill.

3. Peel only the russet potatoes. Slice all the potatoes into roughly 1-inch chunks.

4. Add all the potatoes to the boiling water and cover to cook until tender, about 15 minutes. Drain the potatoes into a colander. Do not rinse!

5. Pour the potatoes into a large bowl. Add the 1 stick butter, 1 tablespoon garlic, 1 tablespoon pepper, 2½ tablespoons salt, the buttermilk, and sour cream.

6. Beat with a hand mixer until the mixture is creamy and dreamy. Do not overmix! There should still be visible lumps of potato. Spoon into a serving dish, mixing in peaks and valleys as you go.

7. Place the butter chips into the valleys and allow to melt just a bit. Dip, serve, and watch it disappear!

A Fabulous Thanksgiving Feast

It's no secret that southerners will hold a get-together to celebrate the opening of an envelope, but there's something about an actual, honest-to-goodness holiday that takes it from a get-together to a full-blown party. No corners are cut and every member of the family's only goal is to outdo everyone else. The ingredients are fresher, the decor gets an upgrade from Dollar Store to Wally World, and the stories about how well each individual family unit is doing are well rehearsed in the freshly scrubbed cars:

> *"Between my promotion, driving the kids to and from sportsball practice, and reading to orphaned iguanas at the ASPCA, I barely had time to harvest my own potatoes, milk the cow, and whip up these Potatoes au Tammy! Have a bite; you can really taste the sacrifice."*

More than that, though, holidays are a time to put all your petty differences aside and share a great meal with everyone . . . until you break into smaller groups, compare notes, and talk shit about the latest gossip from the dinner table!

Fabulous Thanksgiving Feast!

.... ♡ ....

**Without further ado, here it is: your one-stop shop for
a Thanksgiving feast your family will freak out about.**

•

CeeJay's Seriously Good Turkey

•

Good Gravy

•

Sweet Potato Casserole

•

Mama Minj's Savory Corn Bread Stuffing

•

Brussels Sprouts with Bacon

•

Tia's Corn Casserole

•

Pumpkin Spice Old~Fashioned

•

Mac 'n' Cheese Three Ways

•

Cousin Jaime's Bananas Puddin'

•

Kick~Ass Cranberry Sauce

•

Aunt Glenda Faye's Famous Fruit Salad

CeeJay's Seriously Good Turkey

∽ 12 TO 15 SERVINGS ∽

This works best on a standard 15 to 20 pound turkey.

4 to 5 sticks unsalted butter, at room temperature

½ cup chicken or vegetable stock, at room temperature

1 cup dry white wine

1 tablespoon chopped fresh rosemary

1 tablespoon chopped fresh thyme

1 tablespoon chopped fresh sage

2 tablespoons chopped garlic

½ tablespoon granulated garlic

½ tablespoon granulated onion

½ tablespoon salt

½ tablespoon white pepper

1. Put the butter into a stand mixer with the paddle attachment. If you don't have a stand mixer, a standard hand mixer will do. Add the stock slowly until incorporated, then add the wine until incorporated. Mixture will look broken, but that's okay. Next, add the rosemary, thyme, sage, chopped garlic, granulated garlic, granulated onion, salt, and pepper into the mixture. Mix until incorporated.

2. Loosen the skin around the meat of your bird. To do this, gently slide your fingers between the skin and meat, being careful not to pierce the skin. Next, cover the bird with your mixture. Make sure to place some of the mix under the skin of your bird. If you have any left, add to the cavity of the bird.

3. You can search the interwebs for a million different "best" ways to thaw and cook your turkey, but what I have found works best for me is placing the turkey in an aluminum baking dish and allowing it to thaw in the fridge for two days. A lot of people prefer putting it in cold water in the sink, but I've found that takes up too much valuable space and you can't control the temperature! When it comes to cooking your turkey, the general rule of thumb is 13 minutes per pound at 350°F for an unstuffed turkey, or 15 minutes if your bird is stuffed. The internal temperature in the thickest part of the thigh should be 165°F.

Good Gravy

⌣ 15 TO 20 SERVINGS ⌣

3 tablespoons salted butter

3 tablespoons all-purpose flour

1½ cups turkey drippings

1 teaspoon salt

1 teaspoon black pepper

1½ cups chicken stock

1 sprig fresh rosemary

1. Melt the butter over medium heat in a medium saucepan. Use a fork to whisk in your flour, allowing the mixture to brown into a roux.

2. Add the turkey drippings, salt, and pepper to your roux and stir until well mixed. Bring to a boil. Reduce the heat to simmer and slowly mix in the stock. Add the sprig of rosemary, cover, and simmer for about 10 minutes. Remove the rosemary, transfer the gravy to its serving dish, and serve!

Sweet Potato Casserole

⌣ 10 SERVINGS ⌣

5 medium sweet potatoes, peeled and cubed

1 stick butter, melted

1 teaspoon salt

2 large eggs, beaten

½ cup heavy cream

½ cup packed brown sugar

½ teaspoon nutmeg

½ teaspoon cinnamon

¼ teaspoon vanilla extract

2 cups mini marshmallows

1. Preheat the oven to 350°F. Grease a casserole dish generously.

2. Boil the sweet potatoes until tender, about 20 minutes. Drain and cool before transferring to a large mixing bowl.

3. Add the butter, salt, and eggs to the sweet potatoes and use a fork to mash it all together. It's okay if it's a little lumpy! Add the heavy cream, brown sugar, nutmeg, cinnamon, and vanilla, then mix until smooth.

4. Transfer the mixture into the casserole dish, cover evenly with marshmallows, and bake for 25 minutes. Allow to stand for about 25 minutes.

Mama Minj's Savory Corn Bread Stuffing

∽ 15 SERVINGS ∼

FOR THE CORN BREAD

2 cups self-rising cornmeal

3½ teaspoons baking powder

**1 stick unsalted butter,
at room temperature**

Pinch of salt

2 large eggs

1 cup milk

FOR THE STUFFING

Corn bread

1 shredded chicken breast

1 large onion, chopped

3 celery stalks, chopped

6 hard-boiled eggs, chopped

**32-ounce carton chicken
stock, possibly extra for
moisture**

1 teaspoon garlic powder

2 teaspoons poultry seasoning

1 teaspoon celery seeds

2 tablespoons black pepper

Salt (to taste)

MAKE THE CORN BREAD

1. Preheat the oven to 375°F. Generously grease a 9 x 9-inch pan and set aside.

2. Combine the cornmeal, baking powder, butter, and salt in a large mixing bowl and whisk together until well blended. Mix the eggs and milk together in a small bowl and slowly add to your dry mixture, whisking the entire time. Continue to whisk until only a few lumps remain. Pour evenly into your pan and bake for 25 minutes, or until golden brown. Allow to cool overnight to harden a bit.

MAKE THE STUFFING

1. Preheat the oven to 425°F. Grease a large casserole dish.

2. Crumble your corn bread into a fairly even layer of big chunks across the bottom of the casserole dish. Add the chicken, onion, celery, eggs, and stock and mix roughly by hand, making sure to combine the ingredients well. Add the garlic powder, poultry seasoning, celery seeds, and pepper and mix by hand again. Really get in there and squeeze it all together! Taste the mixture and add the salt according to taste. Be mindful that a lot of the seasonings you're using are already salty.

3. Pat the mixture evenly into the casserole dish. If it seems a little soupy, you're on the right track! No one wants a dry stuffing.

4. Bake, uncovered, for about 1 hour, checking for flavor and consistency as you go. If it's too bland, add some salt, mix it up, and continue to bake. If it's too dry, add a little stock, mix well, pat it back down, and continue to bake. It's all up to you! You'll know it's done when there's a nice crust across the top and a knife or toothpick in the middle comes out clean. Allow to cool and serve with a heaping helping of gravy.

Brussels Sprouts with Bacon

⤳ 5 SERVINGS ⤳

1 pound Brussels sprouts

¼ cup olive oil

1 teaspoon salt

2 teaspoons black pepper

⅓ cup cubed, uncooked bacon

¼ cup balsamic vinegar

2 tablespoons honey

1. Preheat the oven to 400°F. Line a baking dish with tinfoil.

2. Clean your sprouts, cut them into halves, and place them in a large mixing bowl. Add the oil, salt, and pepper to the sprouts and toss until well coated. Dump the mixture into the baking dish. Sprinkle the bacon evenly over the top of your mixture.

3. Bake for 25 to 30 minutes, or until the bacon is crispy. Transfer to a bowl and toss with balsamic vinegar and honey.

Tia's Corn Casserole

⤳ 12 SERVINGS ⤳

Nonstick cooking spray

1 stick butter, melted

8.5-ounce package Jiffy corn muffin mix

15.25-ounce can corn, drained

14.75-ounce can cream-style corn

½ cup sour cream

2 large eggs

½ cup granulated sugar

1. Preheat the oven to 350°F and spray a 9 x 9-inch pan with cooking spray. Set aside.

2. In a large mixing bowl combine the butter, corn muffin mix, corn, and creamed corn and mix well. Stir in the sour cream, eggs, and sugar and mix well.

3. Spoon the batter into the pan. Bake for 40 to 45 minutes, or until the center is set. Cut the casserole into squares and serve. Might want to double it all, because it will go fast!

Pumpkin Spice Old-Fashioned

∽ 1 SERVING ∾

FOR THE SIMPLE SYRUP

½ cup water

2 tablespoons brown sugar

1 tablespoon granulated sugar

1½ teaspoons ground cinnamon

½ teaspoon ginger

½ teaspoon allspice

½ teaspoon nutmeg

¼ teaspoon salt

FOR THE DRINK

1 old-fashioned ice cube

¼ cup whiskey of your choice

1 tablespoon pumpkin spice simple syrup

4 dashes orange bitters

1 cinnamon stick (used as a straw!)

1. Combine the water, brown sugar, granulated sugar, ground cinnamon, ginger, allspice, nutmeg, and salt in a small saucepan and whisk until well blended. Bring to a boil. Reduce the heat and simmer for about 5 minutes, whisking occasionally.

2. Remove from the heat and allow to cool before transferring to a jar or other storage container to refrigerate.

3. Add the ice cube to an old-fashioned glass. Pour the whiskey, simple syrup, and orange bitters over the ice cube. Add the cinnamon stick.

Mac 'n' Cheese Three Ways

ABOUT 4 SERVINGS EACH

The true sign of a delicious dish is something you can eat hot out of the oven or from its Tupperware container straight out of the fridge. That was always my granny's mac 'n' cheese. There wasn't much to her recipe and I think it's that simplicity that makes it so addictive!

One Christmas, my cousin Justin and I had gone 'round the block to play with the local kids in Granny's neighborhood, and by the time we got back to the house everyone had already eaten and the food was cold. We had played hard and were starving, so we decided to skip the effort of scooping everything onto a plate and warming it in the microwave. Especially since it was one of those old-school ranges with the giant microwave high above the stove, which required little ole us to drag a chair from the table just to reach it.

We grabbed forks and started eating out of the pots and pans still spread out on the table. The turkey was all dried out, the green bean casserole was goopy, and the biscuits were hard as a rock. But the mac 'n' cheese was soft, buttery, and delicious.

It didn't matter that it was cold, it was everything we needed, and the two of us managed to polish off the rest of the pot with two forks and determination! It's a dish so simple that really hits the spot when you're hungry. And it's so adaptable that you can serve it as a simple side dish or gussy it up for something a little fancier.

GRANNY'S BASIC MAC 'N' CHEESE

2 tablespoons iodized salt

2 tablespoons black pepper

2 cups uncooked elbow macaroni

2 tablespoons salted butter

16-ounce block prepared cheese (such as Velveeta), cubed

⅓ cup milk, warmed

½ teaspoon cayenne pepper

⅓ cup sour cream

1. Put a pot of water on high to boil. Season the water with 1 tablespoon of the salt and 1 tablespoon of the pepper.

2. Add the macaroni and cook until al dente. Drain the pasta into a colander. *Do not rinse.*

3. Pour the pasta back into the pot. Add the butter to the pasta. Mix until melted. Return the pot of buttery pasta to the stove on a low, simmering heat.

4. Add the cheese cubes, warm milk, the remaining 1 tablespoon salt, the remaining 1 tablespoon pepper, and the cayenne. Mix until melted. Add the sour cream, mixing until creamy and blended. Allow to sit for a few minutes to set up. Or don't—it's your call! Just enjoy it!

MAC 'N' CHEESE BALL

Leftover mac that you don't know what to do with? Roll the cold pasta into a ball, flour lightly, dip in a mixture of 1 egg and ½ cup buttermilk, roll in bread crumbs, and fry over medium heat until golden brown for a delicious mac 'n' cheese ball!

FANCY MAC 'N' CHEESE

Want to elevate your dish to impress your friends and family? Mix in 2 cups shredded pork or chicken and ¼ cup diced onions and drizzle ½ cup of your favorite tangy BBQ sauce over the dish. Serve with a spoonful of sour cream right on top and finish with a few chopped scallions. Looks like a million bucks, tastes even better, and takes no time at all!

Cousin Jaime's Bananas Puddin' (This Shit Is Bananas!)

∽ 12 SERVINGS ∾

2 (5.1-ounce) boxes instant vanilla pudding mix

4 cups milk

4 large bananas, sliced

14-ounce can sweetened condensed milk

8-ounce container sour cream

8-ounce container Cool Whip

11-ounce box vanilla wafers

1. Prepare the vanilla pudding mix as instructed on the box (you'll use your milk here). Fold 2 bananas and the condensed milk into the pudding; set aside.

2. Mix the sour cream into the Cool Whip. In a large clear bowl, arrange everything in layers: Cool Whip on the bottom, a layer of bananas above that, crumbled vanilla wafers, then a thick layer of bananas (about twice as thick as the Cool Whip) above that. Repeat until you reach the top of the dish, finishing everything off with a nice layer of the remaining Cool Whip, bananas, and whole vanilla wafers. Refrigerate for at least 1 hour and serve with the biggest spoon you can find!

Kick-Ass Cranberry Sauce

∽ 12 SERVINGS ∾

¾ cup orange juice

¼ cup lemon juice

1 cup granulated sugar

½ teaspoon chopped mint

2 (7-ounce) bags cranberries

1. Combine the orange juice, lemon juice, sugar, and mint in a medium saucepan over medium heat.

2. Once the mixture is well blended and hot, add the cranberries and cook for about 10 minutes, or until the berries begin to pop.

3. Remove from the heat and place in a serving dish. Cool for about 15 minutes before serving.

Aunt Glenda Faye's Famous Fruit Salad

～ ABOUT 10 SERVINGS ～

If there was a competition for fruit salad, Aunt Glenda Faye's would probably be the all-time reigning champion. Even people who hate fruit salad go back for seconds and thirds. There's nothing healthy about it. Yes, there's a ton of fruit in there, but there's also so much sugar and marshmallows and coconut that it becomes a really decadent dessert.

She can no longer make one bowl of this fruit salad. It comes in a giant tray and people will scoop a whole bunch out and they'll take it home and eat from it for the next week.

1 large egg

1 cup granulated sugar

10-ounce jar maraschino cherries, drained (Keep the juice!)

8-ounce can crushed pineapple, drained (Keep the juice!)

2 apples, chopped

2 oranges, segmented

3 bananas, sliced

1 cup green grapes, sliced

1 cup red grapes, sliced

1½ cups mini marshmallows

½ cup sweetened coconut flakes

1. In a small saucepan, whip together the egg, sugar, and juices from the cherries and pineapple until combined and frothy, then cook for 3 to 5 minutes.

2. While your mixture is cooking, combine the cherries, pineapple, apples, oranges, bananas, grapes, marshmallows, and coconut flakes in a large bowl and mix well, taking care not to bruise the fruit. Pour your cooked mixture over the fruit, toss with care, and immediately refrigerate for at least 1 hour. This recipe freezes well if you leave out the bananas.

MAKING AND EDITING
YOUR OWN TRADITIONS

Holiday traditions can be terrific when they're fun and positive for everyone. Maybe there's a particular card game everyone plays after dinner or a tablecloth that everyone signs their names to each year. But sometimes there are traditions we hold on to just because we think we're *supposed* to, even when we don't really enjoy them or they're more effort than they're worth. Sometimes there are bad memories attached, like of family members no longer there. Sometimes the pressure falls all on one person to do all the main cooking or cleaning or decorating, and that person never gets to enjoy the holiday.

You don't have to use that same angel tree topper because it's been in your family for twenty years. That thing is probably falling apart and coated in lead paint. Do you still get all tingly when you pull it out of its storage box? Great—use it. If not, you can let go of the guilt and buy something that you do love now. Decorate with things that represent your favorite places, your favorite characters, your hobbies. And make some of your own ornaments, too—you can use air-dry or oven-baked clay—and get tiny frames for your favorite photos. The more homespun, the better.

Just like I think you should always analyze your life to determine if you could be happier, I think you should do the same with holiday traditions. You're not stuck with them, and they can get stagnant. After my grandmother died, my mom figured she had to make the chicken and dumplings, but she would say, "They never come out as good as when she made them," and then we're all 30 percent less happy, and why is it so important to have chicken and dumplings on that day anyway?

If you decide you want Mexican takeout on Christmas, then you do that. If you don't have any family traditions, spend some time thinking about how to make some.

7
·Becoming a ·Lady

The stereotypical idea of "being a lady" means being well-groomed and docile and the secondary character in someone else's story. But that didn't fit the ladies I grew up around. Even the church ladies always spoke their mind—it's just that they could tell you to eat shit and die in such beautiful, buttery-tongued ways that you'd say, "Thank you."

When I think about my vision of a lady, it's this: A lady carries herself like she's proud of who she is. I don't care if she's in a Laura Ingalls Wilder dress or a bikini in the grocery store; she holds her head high. A lady speaks up and speaks out truthfully, but in ways meant to be constructive, not hitting below the belt. She's careful with her words and aware of her surroundings so she can figure out what's appropriate in different environments. Ladies respect themselves and their worth. They take others into account, but they also don't allow themselves to become anyone's props.

They reveal what they choose to about themselves and won't be pressured into inviting judgment. When someone asked my aunt Glenda when she graduated from high school, she said, "My senior year."

Ladies—all ladies—are beautiful. Even you. I mean, your ears are kind of big, but *love you. Mean it.*

I had lots of fantasies in my mind about being a lady and I playacted them, but I didn't have a chance to fully embody the art of drag until I started working in improv dinner theatre.

In 2007, I was working as the costumer for the Starlight Dinner Theatre in Orlando, a real ramshackle operation. I loved the owner, but she wasn't business minded and kept putting me in messy situations—I'd order a bunch of costumes from another theatre for a show and she'd cancel the order without telling me because she didn't have enough money in the budget. So then I'd be cutting up and hand-painting banquet tablecloths for *Guys and Dolls* at the last minute because we had no real costumes.

What I really wanted to do was be in the shows, but the owner wouldn't allow staff to do both. There was too much turnover and she needed me as a costumer more than she needed another performer.

While working there, I saw an audition notice for a play called *boys, boys, boys!* to be featured at the Orlando Fringe Festival—one of those "anyone who's anyone will be there" kinds of uncensored theatrical events that attracted interesting people from all over the world. The play was based on a real bar in New York City in the 1970s, which had a gay burlesque show that also featured nude male dancers. The director was looking for eight male actors willing to go completely naked, and two drag queens.

Well, even "tasteful nudity" was not something anywhere near my comfort zone, so those parts were out, but I figured I could try out for one of the queens. I'd *kind of* done drag before for Halloween and some special events at the bar . . . at least, I thought I had done drag. What I'd really done was put on a wig and some drugstore lipstick and eyeliner, which is not the same thing at all, but I didn't know then that there was more to it. Being a lady is a lot more than lipstick and teasing combs, and drag is about heightening femininity to an extreme art.

Anyhoo, I tried out and I got cast. In the show, there's a twenty-year time jump and older actors are looking back on their younger selves. I was cast as the younger version of drag queen Rusti Fawcett, who took me under his wing and taught me about the real artistry of drag makeup and costuming.

"I'm going to be your drag mother," he announced, which sounded good to me. What he did was something I'll never forget: He did makeup on only one half of my face. I sat there expectantly and finally asked, "What about the other half?"

"I can paint you to look beautiful for one night, but you're not going to learn anything. And I'm not always going to be there to paint your face. So now you try to match what I did on the other side."

It was a perfect exercise. Before he did that, I had no concept of blending or shading or contouring, creating new eyebrow lines or eyelid creases. I tried hard to make my side look

DRAG MAKEUP AND WOMEN

I can't go anywhere without a woman asking me to do her makeup. Drag makeup, though, is so different from up-close-and-personal–type makeup for your everyday woman. Men usually have lower brow lines, more pronounced jawlines, just different bone structure that needs to be contoured differently, and our makeup is designed for stage lighting and viewing from more distance— which means it can look really spackled on and overdone up close.

But what women can take from the drag world is the Neapolitan ice cream look: brown, pink, and white. Those are really the only three colors you need on top of your foundation. The brown is your contour (bottom of your cheeks), the white is your highlighter (top of your cheeks), and the pink is your warm tone (middle). Those three colors work on all skin tones, and you can use them to create shapes and shadows across your nose, forehead, chin, neck, everywhere. You have to play with placement to figure out what works with your facial structure, but don't worry if you literally look like Neapolitan ice cream when you first apply it—it all works itself out in the blending!

You can also take screenshots of yourself with your favorite filters on Snapchat or wherever—and then get in front of a mirror and figure out what those filters are doing and try to copy them.

One common mistake people make is in contouring their noses: The widest part should be the bridge, between your eyes, and then you pull it down to a tip a good quarter inch or so above where the actual tip of your nose is. So you're basically drawing a long triangle downward. A lot of people do the opposite, and then their noses look bulbous and they don't understand why. But now you know, so your nose is going to look fucking fantastic.

just like the side he'd done, which was harder than I expected—I looked like I was mid-stroke and half of my face was melting downward, but it forced me to spend time working on it and learning better makeup techniques, before YouTube tutorials were a thing.

"Foundation is the key to everything," he told me. "Just like with a house, if you build on cheap foundation, everything crumbles. You can't go to the store and buy liquid Maybelline. 'Maybe' is the first part of the brand name. Maybe it's gonna cover, maybe not. And chances are if you can get it for five dollars it's not going to cover."

I balked at the price of the foundation Rusti wanted me to buy at a specialty store, but he was adamant about it. "If you buy this twenty-five-dollar foundation, I can teach you how to make all of the cheap cosmetics work on top of it."

So I bought the foundation and then we headed to the dollar store, where they had a Jordana makeup collection priced between $1 and $1.50. We picked bright colors because he told me the brighter the color, the heavier the pigment, so you use less and don't go through it as quickly if you get red eye shadow instead of mauve.

Fringe Festival was the first time I'd ever performed in drag, and it was a big success. My show had beloved queens who'd been on the scene forever, and Disney performers whom people showed up to see; it was this big, talented cast that I was lucky to be thrown into, and we got a lot of attention. I was the "exciting new discovery" who reaped the benefits of their hard work. Afterward, several people offered me gigs, including Sleuths Mystery Dinner Shows. Rusti worked there and introduced me to the co-owner, Sandy Redmond. She said, "You've been costuming at Starlight, right? We could really use some help with that, too, if you want to come and perform with us."

"Are you saying I can do both?"

"Yes."

"Sign me up."

Sleuths was a terrific atmosphere. It was a long-running part-scripted and part-improv comedy show where a small cast revealed clues about who committed a murder and the audience had to make a guess about whodunit while they were eating their meal. It rotated four different shows each week so that guests could come more than one night in the same week and see a different show.

One of the fun parts for me was that, because it was a small cast, we each played all sorts of different roles. Some male roles, some female roles. So I got to exercise my drag skill in this new, supportive environment. It was a popular tourist attraction and a lot of fun to interact with an audience in such an up-close way . . . we were directly walking through the tables and talking with people throughout the performances, teasing people about their Mickey Mouse clothes or their dates. Everyone had a great time. It was the kind of work I loved to do; it was creative and a little different every night, and gave me lots of opportunity to improve my craft.

One of the other perks was the connections it gave me. So many times, a nightclub manager would come see our show and invite me to come perform at the club, or a pageant promoter would say, "Come do our pageant!" It moved me further and further into the real drag world instead of just the theatrical version of it. But for some time, I was very happily doing both, and then some.

I took over as the costumer at Sleuths because Gidget Galore was leaving to start her own costume shop. She helped me get acquainted there, and we ended up becoming the best of friends. We're polar opposites, but that's part of the joy of it. Another of my best friends and the most talented person I've ever met, Janine, worked at Sleuths with me and we'd get tipsy off wine spritzers before the show. We needed someone like Gidget to balance us out and lead us in the right direction so we didn't fly off the rails and just become drunken bitchy queens.

I also got to meet drag legend Carmella Marcella Garcia, "The Grand Ole Gal of the South," who came by often to see her drag sister Rusti. Carmella took my breath away; whereas drag was a job to Rusti, it was a calling for Carmella. She was someone I looked up to and felt a kinship with; the more I got to know her, the more mesmerizing I found her—she was fat and beautiful and sexy and knew what to do with her body, *and* she was smart and funny and raw and everybody loved her.

She was multitalented as a country and jazz singer, pianist, stand-up comedian, and drag queen. She could read you to *filth* and make you laugh about it because as bitchy as she was, she was also full of love and good intentions.

Rusti was styling the wigs and I was working on the costumes in those days, and Carmella would come by and say, "Here's the new way to style a bang that I just learned when I was in Nashville. And here's the new way to curl a wig, which I just learned in Louisville. And if you use lemon Pledge on old wigs, that makes them shine."

"You really do everything," I said to her. "You're an actress and a director and a producer and a writer and a costumer. . . ."

"Yeah, I grew up doing theatre," she said. "I didn't like people telling me how to do my art, so I figured out a way to do it on my own."

"This is what I should be doing," I thought. She was putting together all these Broadway one-woman shows, and she was so driven to create. I wanted to be just like her. Until she told me not to.

We were brushing out wigs at Sleuths when she said, "Find your own path, bitch, and stop trying to steal mine."

Well, that stung. "I'm not trying to. I just love you so much."

"Yeah, and there are lots of other drag queens I love, too, but I learned that when I started being honest about who I was and what I wanted to do and what I was capable of doing, then other people got on board. So that's all I'm telling you. You can emulate me and you can idolize me—I don't mind—but try to do *you*."

It's when I applied her advice that I really started to find success. I had to learn that just because floral minidresses worked on Carmella didn't mean they were for me, and that little kitten heels like hers made me look too matronly. I had to learn that I felt best in a red wig and stilettos, and that I could tell my stories my own way without trying to copy her comedic timing. And even if there were pieces of Carmella's look and act and pathway that I wanted to hold on to, I also had instincts that I had to trust about how to entertain an audience.

I'm not afraid to drop an f-bomb, but I felt most comfortable as a "sophisticated clown." Someone who is risqué enough for the adults, but who knows how to tell jokes that won't make you feel uncomfortable if your kids are in the room because the innu-endos fly right over their heads. When you do something that's authentic to you, I think that reads to the room.

Mentors are like training wheels; you rely on them for support until you're steady enough to ride on your own. When I started out, I was using other people's dresses and jokes, but over time it becomes more of an homage—there's always a little of everyone who taught me along the way, just like there's a little Ginger in everyone I've ever . . . taught . . . along the way.

Poisoned Apple Fizz

⟶ 1 SERVING ⟵

When one wants to be very, very ladylike, I believe one should have a very, very lady-like drink that gives them the urge to take kissy-face selfies.

½ tablespoon cinnamon

½ tablespoon granulated sugar

½ tablespoon Tajín

½ ounce caramel syrup

2 ounces apple vodka

3 ounces prosecco

1 ounce Sour Apple Pucker

¼ teaspoon lime juice

Apple slice (for garnish)

1. Mix the cinnamon, sugar, and Tajín in a bowl. Drizzle the caramel syrup around the rim of a glass and dust with your rimming mixture.

2. Shake the vodka, prosecco, Sour Apple Pucker, and lime juice with ice. Strain into the glass, garnish with a slice of apple, and serve!

The Birth of Ginger Minj

It was there at Sleuths that my drag character was born and developed and named, and I owe it to Sandy.

I'd been working on my drag, taking inspiration from a few places: primarily the gossipy church ladies around my hometown, with their "the bigger the hair, the closer to Jesus" lewks; and the comedy flair of Lucille Ball and Carol Burnett. I adore both of them because they were these gorgeous women who looked glamorous and ladylike but would not be afraid to fall down some stairs or get a pie in the face in the name of comedy. They weren't afraid to get ugly, and I enjoyed that so much.

Divine, too. I never set out to emulate Divine's style, though people will put us in the same box just because of our body types. But I wanted to be that kind of self-confident and that devoted to creating a character that would make people pay attention.

When I started out, I hadn't settled on a name—I was just using my own name. Sandy offered to sponsor me for my first drag pageant, and she suggested the name Ginger Minj because of an earlier *incident* at Sleuths. During an ad-libbing part of the show, one of the male actors had pointed out a redhead in the audience and said to another actor, "Hey, Nigel, do you think this one's got a ginger minge?"

Well . . . in case you don't know this yet (and if that's the case, I'm sorry in advance for spoiling your innocence), "minge" is British slang for "vagina." It turned out the woman was British, knew just what he meant, and punched the actor in the face, breaking his jaw in front of everyone.

Which is horrendous, of course, but also the stuff of legends. I thought the name was perfect for so many reasons—it gave a nod to Sleuths, which was really the starting ground of my career, and it sounded classy if you didn't know what it meant.

So that was me. Red-haired Vagina. Now that I had a name, it felt more real. This drag work that I was doing "on the side" felt more and more like what I was actually meant to do.

DON'T LET YOUR SKIN LOOK LIKE SHIT

I'm going to let you in on a secret: Lots of drag queens' skin is a mess in person. When you put on the layers and layers of makeup that we do and leave it on for hours at a time under heavy lights, you have to do a lot to counteract that or it'll just leave your skin dried out, full of acne, and irritated all the time. But you don't have to be a queen to follow my skin care routine; it's what everyone should be doing if they want their face to look its best.

Makeup needs a smooth canvas. When your skin is messed up, the makeup has a harder job to do and you're going to see the texture of every lump and bump. So here's what I suggest:

Wash off your makeup every night with steam to open your pores and get everything out. Don't just use makeup wipes, which dry out your skin and aren't as thorough. Keep your skin hydrated with high-quality moisturizer, and wear foundation with SPF if you're going outdoors. It's way harder to undo sun damage than to avoid it in the first place.

If you're prone to under-eye bags or wrinkles, use a hydrogel under-eye mask. I sleep with mine, even though you're probably not supposed to do that.

Use facial masks every week. I use three of them each week:

First a mask that draws everything out of my pores, generally a foaming charcoal mask.

Two days later, a nourishing mud mask that hardens and then rinses off.

At the end of the week, a hydration mask that stays on my skin—I prefer not to use sheet masks because I think too much of the product stays on the sheet and doesn't get absorbed.

Don't just keep using the same kind of mask; there are different kinds with different functions, and the idea is basically to trick your skin into being healthy—first you're pulling things out; then you're putting moisture back in. And then your skin won't look like shit. Ta-da!

MAKEUP DOS AND DON'TS FOR REAL LIFE

DO

* Combine eye shadow with a little 91 percent isopropyl alcohol and swish it around with your brush to create a paste to make it more pigmented and longer lasting for dramatic effects.

* Use continuous fine mist setting spray.

* Glitter. It covers all kinds of mistakes if you have uneven lines or edges on your eyelids.

* Put mascara on both before and after applying fake lashes.

* Learn what size eyelashes fit you best (for me, it's 304s), and then as the glue dries shape them upward with your fingers so they don't hang down on the corners.

* Keep your face powder on for several minutes before dusting it off. Let it absorb any oil and shine from your makeup.

DON'T

* Contour so much that you look like Skeletor; what works onstage doesn't work in regular life.

* Use setting spray that contains alcohol—it dries out your skin and doesn't work any better than the ones without alcohol.

* Skimp on lip liner. It's one of the few things I spend real money on because it's important to find one that doesn't feather and will stay on. Outline and then darken the outer areas of the lips.

* Forget to take lighting into account! Just like gowns, there are different styles of makeup to complement different environments. What elicits "oohs!" and "ahhs!" of desire in a dark bar at 2:00 a.m. will most likely achieve the opposite effect at an up-close brunch at noon!

* Try to look like anyone else. I cannot stress this enough. You are your own unique brand of beautiful and what works for someone else may make you look like you just crawled backwards out of a well and into someone's TV.

The Naughty Wall

Divine was the first drag role model I ever had, starting when I was nine or ten years old. Between my school and my grandparents' house, there was this gas station that was also a barbecue restaurant and also a video store, and my granny would let me pick out the videos we'd watch each weekend. There were two walls I was allowed to pick from, and then there was the R-rated wall that I was not allowed to pick from, and then there was the stuff behind the curtain in the back that I was *really* not allowed to pick from.

I mostly stuck to my two walls, but I kept spotting this title on the R-rated wall: *Pink Flamingos*. I don't know what drew me to it because it didn't even have cover art, but something made me want to grab it. One day I did, and when my granny asked about it I said it was a cartoon. She believed it.

That night after she went to bed, I took the combo TV/VCR onto the couch and I pulled a quilt over it and myself, and I watched *Pink Flamingos* on the lowest possible volume. I had no idea what the hell it was about. I still have no idea what the hell it's about. Have you seen it? No one knows what the hell it's about. But I knew one thing: I loved these weird misfit characters, especially Divine.

She was the first drag queen I'd ever seen, and I didn't realize at first that she wasn't biologically female. I thought she was a woman with masculine features, and when I learned otherwise I was fascinated. She wasn't conventionally pretty, but I thought she was beautiful, with her over-the-top makeup and style. She was a legitimate movie star who died before her time, just nine days after *Hairspray* was released in 1988. I think of her now as the Marilyn Monroe of the drag world, someone who created her own image and died just as her star was shining its brightest. She had much more to give.

I started looking for other movies like that. *Polyester* was my favorite. And I watched interviews with her, which revealed a much more subdued person than the characters she played. I thought it was so refreshing to see someone who wasn't like what people thought she should be, and to do it so unashamedly and so successfully.

When I felt alone as a child, Divine got me through. I looked at her and thought, "I'm not the only one like me in the world." Even if I didn't understand what drag was all about, Divine helped me realize that somewhere on earth there was a place where people could appreciate a feminine boy. I drew a great deal of strength from her. When

I started doing drag, I hoped I could someday provide that same kind of role model for another kid growing up queer.

One of the things drag did for me was to let me explore my feminine feelings in a safe way. The more I got into it, the more I wondered if maybe I was trans. It took some time for me to work through that thought, to figure out if I felt like I actually *was* a woman, and not someone who liked to dress and paint myself like one. There was a lot I related to about womanhood, not just because I love the look of femininity but also because I always felt like a nurturer, a softer spirit.

But there was the Joshua part of me, too.

I wasn't Ginger all the time; that didn't feel right either. So where did I fit? The terms "nonbinary" and "genderqueer" weren't around in my youth, but when I learned what they meant that's what I settled into: I didn't feel fully male *or* female, but something of a combination of the two. As for pronouns, I usually call myself and my drag sisters she unless told otherwise, but I accept any pronouns that are used with good intent.

Drag Queen Muffins (Okay, Cupcakes!)

⌒ 12 SERVINGS ⌒

In every facet of my life, I strive to be a good hostess, whether that's onstage or at home when I invite people over. Part of the joy of cooking for me is having people enjoy their experience in my home, so I want to make them comfortable. I want to make sure it smells good, looks good, that the conversation is good, and that definitely everything they put in their mouth is delicious—whether that be my food or another guest at the end of the night.

Regular cupcakes are lovely, but they're just kind of there. With drag queen cupcakes, they're going to taste delicious, but you're also putting the polish on—the shine to make them visually appealing. And if you decorate them right, they're a conversation starter.

FOR THE MUFFINS

1⅓ cups vegetable oil

2 cups granulated sugar

3 large eggs, beaten

3 cups all-purpose flour

1 teaspoon salt

1 teaspoon baking soda

2 tablespoons vanilla extract

1 cup fresh fruit (I prefer blueberries!)

FOR THE SOFT SOUTHERN ICING

1 cup milk

4½ tablespoons all-purpose flour

1 cup granulated sugar

1½ sticks butter, at room temperature

1 teaspoon vanilla extract

Dash of salt

Edible glitter of your choice, nonpareils, and candy of your choice (I like to put candy charm bracelets at the base of the cupcakes and then go wild with candy jewelry and sugar eyes)

MAKE THE MUFFINS

1. Preheat the oven to 325°F. Line a 12-cupcake tin with paper liners.

2. Mix the oil and sugar well in a large bowl. Add your eggs into the mixture. Gradually stir in the flour, salt, baking soda, and vanilla. This is a good place to add in any fresh fruits you might like, such as strawberries, blueberries, apples, et cetera. Go wild! The fresh fruit adds a lot of moisture to your cake.

3. Use an ice-cream scoop to add the batter to your cupcake tin and bake for 45 minutes, or until golden brown. Remove from the tin and allow to cool before decorating.

MAKE THE SOFT SOUTHERN ICING

1. Blend the milk and flour until smooth. Cook over low heat until very thick and stiff. Set aside to cool. This mixture *must* be cool before continuing!

2. Cream together the sugar, butter, vanilla, and salt with an electric mixer on high speed. Add the cooled flour-milk mixture a spoonful at a time, beating between each addition. Chill the mixture before icing your cake.

3. Drag queens are known for taking chances and really bringing the fabulous, so go over the top! Pipe that icing higher than a 1990s pageant updo, sprinkle it with edible glitter and nonpareils, and top it off with a sexy piece of candy jewelry (rings, bracelets, earrings, necklaces . . . they've got everything, even lipsticks!).

Now, one of the main barriers to drag is that it's expensive to do it right. If you're just messing around, sure, you can go to the mall and try some shit on and just wear whatever sort of fits and whatever cheap wigs you find online, but not if you're trying to get taken seriously as a pageant girl or a performer. Then you need a customized wardrobe, fitted to your body, and high-quality wigs that don't look like you got them in a drugstore's seasonal aisle, along with makeup, shoes, nails, lashes, accessories, padding, breast forms, plus little extra things like glue for your eyebrows (unless you shave them off), safety pins, bobby pins, hairspray, and duct tape for everything. Everything.

My next book is going to be *1001 Uses for Duct Tape*, but here's your teaser:

* Tucks. Yes, we use duct tape to tuck, and yes, it's a bitch to pull it off. I don't tuck unless I have to, and then I take it off in a hot, steamy shower afterward.

* Bottoms of shoes for traction.

* Inside shoes so your pantyhose doesn't stick.

* Around your face (attached over your wig cap) for a do-it-yourself facelift.

So the tricky thing about drag is that you need money to make money, especially if you're doing pageants or *Drag Race*, both of which require you to have a multitude of finished looks. When I was getting started, one of the main reasons I created the character as I did was that my original version of Ginger was more of a southern church lady and I could buy cheap suits at Ross for her. Then I just piled curly hair wigs on top of my head and threw a flower on top.

And the thing about it is that characters aren't just for drag performers—you get to choose to be your own character every day. If you want to up your drama factor, you can do the same thing—get some clip-in hair extensions or a wig (they weren't invented for drag queens; we just perfected them), tease it up (the higher the hair, the lower the morals), stick a marabou feather clip in it, put on that red lipstick . . . keep playing with your own look until you feel like your "character" matches how you feel best. If you're considering a drastic change of cut or color, buy a twenty-dollar wig on Amazon and try it out to see if you like it before you cut your own hair. Or don't—screw it, it grows back. Usually. Whatever you do, do it with conviction.

As I got paid, I reinvested it in my drag. So now Ginger has three bedrooms in my house and I have one. Being a lady is a *commitment*, y'all.

What I discovered in drag was an acceptance and a community. Which is not to say that it was a smooth path; I've had to fight to prove myself because I don't look like the girls who normally get regular jobs.

Early on, I made a portfolio of my drag looks and typed up a bio and began sending it out to nightclubs. There was a belief in the community that lesbians and gay men didn't get along—they had their own separate bars—and that lesbians didn't like drag because they thought it was misogynistic. So queens were not promoting themselves to lesbian bars. But I did because that belief never made any sense to me—and what amazed me was that they were the first ones responding.

"No one ever wants to come entertain here," one of the owners told me. "We'd love to talk to you."

My first paid show was at a lesbian bar called Faces in Orlando, and they gave me a tiny piece of their budget, but it was enough to bring in a couple of my friends and create a show once a week. There was no dressing room and no stage, so we changed in a shed out back and performed on the dance floor. We worked to build it up, and sure enough, after a while we began attracting a crowd—not just lesbians, but a diverse mix of people who started showing up and getting along and having fun with us. Then the nightclub Pulse reached out to me and asked me to perform, just for tips.

A lot of girls expect to get paid the moment they put a wig on their head, and I'm a strong proponent of knowing what you're worth and going after it—but I'm also a fan of working your way up until you have something valuable to bring to the table. My friends and I weren't so worried about money then; we wanted to get our names out and polish our act. Pulse was a beautiful place to perform, and several *Drag Race* girls came through there: Roxxxy Andrews was literally the face of Pulse—there's a giant portrait of her on the wall, probably ten feet tall. Detox, Coco Montrese, and Tyra Sanchez were all regulars, and they were welcoming to us.

But eventually I realized that no one was going to give me regular paid jobs if I didn't create them for myself. Orlando's drag scene called for thin body types, and most of the popular queens were trans women. My friends were a bunch of merry misfits, who would all get shoved to the side by the current people in power. Talented enough to perform from time to time in our own group, but not who they wanted to represent them in any official way.

So I applied for a job at Bananas Modern American Diner, which employed drag servers. You'd serve food and do numbers in between. When they said they'd hire me, I said, "I'll do it as long as you'll give me one night a week where I can do a Broadway-themed drag show with my friends."

"That'll never fly here," one of the owners told me.

"This town has one of the most thriving theatre communities anywhere, and nobody caters to them," I told him.

"Well, I don't think it's going to work, but you can have Tuesdays. That's our worst night."

"I'll take what I can get."

It was an immediate success, and demand was so high that we expanded it to a longer set and then added on more nights: first two nights a week, and then three. The reaction rivaled when I used to dance on the top of my grandparents' bar: I felt such love and support from the community. They *got* it—they loved what I did, and it made me feel ten feet tall. I was doing what Carmella told me to do: finding my own path, staying authentic to what I loved and where I came from. And she was right: People were responding to it.

When Bananas closed down, my friends and I took the act to Hamburger Mary's, where it's still running today even without me. I swear that more than any other accomplishment, my legacy is going to be that Sunday Broadway Brunch at Hamburger Mary's. Go see it sometime.

8
Southern Drama

Why say it in twenty words when you can say it in two hundred words? Southern theatre is descriptive and expansive. So okay, the North has Lin-Manuel Miranda, but we claim Tennessee Williams and Lillian Hellman, who both wrote about southern settings and southern people in ways that would immortalize southern culture. You can always count on family drama, messy characters, overflowing emotion, macabre humor, repressed sexuality, and insistence on impeccable manners.

Cat on a Hot Tin Roof gets to the essence of southern families—you have love, hate, violence, and everything in between, with food as the through-line. They find every opportunity to describe what they're going to eat. Much like in my real life, the only time the characters shut up and stop fighting with one another is when they're going to eat dinner. I think that may be why southern food is so heavy, too, because you just want to tire everybody out so they don't have the energy to drive you crazy anymore. Where else in the world do you get up in the morning and eat biscuits covered with bread gravy, sausage, grits, with a side of toast and potatoes? By the time you eat it, you're ready to go back to sleep.

I once played one of the no-neck monsters in a production, but I wanted to be Maggie so badly because I understood the idea of feeling like a cat on a hot tin roof—having so much energy and intention but being held back and scorched by your surroundings. It's always been one of my favorites.

Theatre has always felt like home to me because of the way it provides a place for stories to be told. It's such a human endeavor, to want to act out scenarios that other people can relate to—love, heartbreak, loss, following dreams, finding our places in

MAKE THEM SEE YOU LIKE YOU SEE YOU

We'd never make any social progress if shows were cast exactly as they've always been done and we all just went along with whatever a director's first impression was. In theatre and in life, you have to be willing to stand out and to ask for what you need.

Sometimes that means asking for another shot because you know you can do better. Sometimes it means asking, "Can I read for this other role?" Sometimes it means showing up for roles even when you know you're not the typical type—as long as you know you can pull it off. Ado Annie in *Oklahoma!* wasn't written as a wheelchair user, but Ali Stroker won a Tony Award for her portrayal.

If you go for roles that are out of your singing range or where your physicality will make no sense with the script, then you're just wasting everyone's time. But if you have a different spin on a character and you know it's worth seeing, then do what it takes to get that opportunity. Sure, sometimes directors won't deviate from whatever vision they have in mind, but sometimes they don't know until you get there that they were actually looking for *you*.

And I don't mean that in just an acting sense. That goes for things like applying to long-shot colleges because you know there's something special you have to offer beyond your GPA, or writing to a hiring manager in Delaware and saying: "I know you're looking for in-office staff, but I can do this remotely and I have all these great ideas for your company." One of the things that always drive me crazy is hearing the feedback "You're overqualified" for a job. Bitch, if I'm here, I don't think it's beneath me, so why make that judgment for me? Don't be afraid to advocate for yourself, whether that means explaining

the world, realizing we have green skin and maybe our mother fucked a traveling elixir salesman.

Acting gives you a break from reality; for a while, you can try on a whole new life, and that's something many of us could use. With theatre you get to play out whole emotional arcs from beginning to end, whereas with film and television you might film a scene one day and then a prior scene two days later, all piecemeal and disjointed, and never even see the full performance until it's finished and edited. I love film and TV, of course (*hire me okay thanks*), but I always come back to the theatre because I would feel like an unfinished person without it.

There's this immediacy to it when you can feel an audience laughing with you, smiling, leaning forward in their chairs, and applauding for you. Nobody does that because why your overqualifications are a good thing or why your underqualifications won't hold you back.

Were it up to my managers, I wouldn't have been in the movie *Dumplin'*. They didn't submit me for it. They submitted lots of skinny *Drag Race* girls, but not me. I was hanging around the office and read parts of the script and loved it. So often, filmmakers want to put drag queens in their movies, but they don't actually know what to do with us, so you wind up with this total straight white man version of what he thinks drag sounds like: "Yes, sister, work it! You better slay me all day, hunty!" It's a minstrel show. On the one hand, you're glad for the opportunities (because otherwise they'll just go to straight cis men who make a mockery of drag), and on the other, it's hard to see yourself as a fully realized individual when the world keeps seeing you this way.

Dumplin' was better than that, so I googled to find out where to submit an audition tape myself.

On it, I said: "My management company didn't put me up for this. You didn't ask me to audition. And I think that's bullshit, because this story is my story. If you want somebody who relates to these characters, it's going to be me."

Not only did I get the part, but they also expanded it for me. I got prominent billing in the movie's advertisements, which was almost embarrassing because it made it look like I was starring along with Jennifer Aniston. That was a teensy bit overstating it. But still! I was in a hit mainstream movie, and my management company learned not to doubt me.

When you know something should be yours, don't sit back and wait for someone to figure that out and offer it to you. Knock on those doors and invite yourself in.

you're good at math. You could do all the quadratic equations in the world and still never experience a standing ovation, which is a shame, really, because good for you. Quadratic equations are hard.

Back when Sherry convinced me to join the children's theatre, I lucked out: Our first big production was *The Wizard of Oz*, my favorite movie. I knew I could play a Munchkin because I was short and Munchkin shaped, and I figured I would feel comfortable in a group. But then they showed us the costumes, and I loved the Mayor of Munchkin City's costume, which made me decide to audition.

I sang my part quietly, and then the kid next to me stood up and belted it out off-key. It was terrible, but the directors were laughing and having such a good time because he was entertaining. Well, that ignited something in me, and I asked, "Can I do it again?"

Deborah said I could, so I got up there and I gave it everything I had this time. I was loud and animated, and she flipped. "When did you become Ethel Merman?"

I didn't know that was a compliment until I found out I got the part.

I was just twelve or so the first time I went on tour. Not like the big national tours that follow Broadway shows, just a couple weeks at a time on school breaks and summers. My children's theatre group had gone to nursing homes and local elementary schools to perform fairy tales, and then we did a mainstage performance of *Joseph and the Amazing Technicolor Dreamcoat* that was such a runaway hit we couldn't move on to the next show—we just had to keep adding performances because it kept selling. It won Best in Show at the Florida Theatre Conference, and we were invited to perform all over the state.

Then we did *Oliver!* I was originally cast as Oliver, but I started going through my pubescent voice drop, so they switched my role to the Artful Dodger. That's one of the dangers of working as a kid actor—there are even "growth spurt" clauses in professional contracts. Like, if you grow more than an inch, they toss you out like yesterday's muffins. I was lucky they had a backup role for me.

We'd go on bus and truck tours with these bigger shows, staying four kids and a chaperone per room at motels along the way. It was so much fun, and helped me see past my horizons.

What I started learning then was about the repetitiveness of professional theatre, which is different from school shows. In school, you perform a show for one or two weekends and it's over. Professionally, you might play the same role in the same show for years, five times a week, and each time you have to find a way to make it feel just as energetic and fresh as the first time. Always changing little nuances, always trying to make it better for the people who come back. Some kids would get bored of that and go back to just doing school shows, but not me—I enjoyed the challenge of making something old into something new.

As I got older, I aged out of the children's shows and began doing more professional tours. There was no money in it, but we felt like real actors. I was taking control of what I wanted to do with my life, and that was empowering.

Honest-to-Goodness Southern Fried Chicken

⌒ 3 TO 4 SERVINGS ⌒

Behold, the most southern dish in the world. Just like southerners, it's a little extra. There's an element of drama to good southern cooking because it takes preparation and care: You're not just going to throw a chicken in the oven and call it good. You're going to prepare it overnight and dress it up and make sure it comes out ready to dazzle!

1 whole chicken, cut into pieces

½ gallon buttermilk

3 cups vegetable oil

1 cup all-purpose flour

1 tablespoon paprika

⅓ cup black pepper

2 tablespoons salt

1 tablespoon dill

½ tablespoon cumin

1. Before you begin cooking, soak your chicken overnight in a bowl of buttermilk in the fridge.

2. Heat the oil over medium-high heat in a deep large skillet.

3. Mix the flour, paprika, pepper, salt, dill, and cumin in a brown paper lunch bag. Shake until well mixed.

4. Piece by piece, add the chicken to the bag, close, and shake until well coated. Place the battered pieces on a baking sheet and set aside.

5. Work in batches, a few pieces at a time, frying the chicken in the skillet. Be sure not to overcrowd the skillet. Turn the chicken so that all sides fry golden brown and even. Chicken will be done when the juices run clear and the internal temperature reaches 165°F, anywhere between 10 and 15 minutes for smaller pieces and 15 and 20 minutes for breasts.

6. Place the cooked chicken on a tray lined with paper towels to absorb any excess grease. Allow to cool and serve!

Leaving Home

I was eighteen when I came to a crossroads in my life: I was running the children's theatre program, which everyone assumed was going to be my long-term job. Only two people had ever run the program since the 1970s and they were handing the reins over to me. But as much as I enjoyed it, I was dreaming about making it to Broadway. My friend Adrian said, "Why don't we just do it? Now?"

I thought about it for a minute and decided, "If I don't do it now, I might never." Because really, what better time is there? We all spend so much of our lives waiting for the perfect timing, and I worried that the roots I was growing at the theatre were going to keep me shackled to my little hometown forever.

I turned the children's program over to someone else, and one week later Adrian and I headed to New York City with the $5,000 we saved up. That would be plenty to last me a few months, I figured. I'd sold my car, but only crazy people and cabdrivers drive in New York City. (There is some overlap.)

I showed up with no job and no place to stay, and was quickly smacked in the face by the reality of housing in New York—the same money that could rent me a whole house in Florida was the cost of a single room in someone else's apartment in Washington Heights. And that was just the rent; every other cost—food, transportation, utilities—was also astronomical. So I quickly came to understand why it was the city that never sleeps: No one could afford to sleep!

I went knocking on doors and begging for work, and finally found a job in merchandising for *Beauty and the Beast* on Broadway. It wasn't full-time, though—it was shift work whenever I could pick it up—so I also worked two other part-time jobs with irregular hours, and I still couldn't make ends meet.

The problem was that between all my jobs, I never had time to audition or even to take lessons. I was supposed to be working these jobs until I got my big break, but there was no space for that big break to happen.

One positive thing was that I began performing with the *Beauty and the Beast* cast at special events. Disney had a wonderful policy that anyone in the company could perform with the cast at benefits and promotional events like Broadway Cares and Equity Fights AIDS, and I got lucky one day when several cast members called in sick—they gave me several solo lines, and that improved my standing. From that point on, I was often featured during these events.

I didn't have my Actors' Equity Association card, which meant that I couldn't try out for the show itself yet—you have to be a member of the union to audition, and that usually means working your way up at regional Equity theatres first. I was more than willing to put in the effort, but I couldn't afford to take the risk of quitting my other jobs for a short-lived show just for the hope that it would then get my foot in the door for Broadway.

At eighteen, I just wasn't emotionally or financially prepared for New York City, but that doesn't mean I didn't try. I did, for three years. I dated an older man there, I made friends, I enjoyed working on two different Broadway shows—*Lion King* being the second, where I worked in merchandising and costuming—and I tried hard to figure out a way to make things happen.

I also got kidnapped. As I was walking home one night, a guy asked me if I had a cigarette and I said, "No, sorry," and then as I turned to walk away realized he'd put a gun to my back.

"I need your money," he said. And in my moment of abject brilliance, I said, "I don't have any money. All I have is my paycheck."

Well, he was delighted to hail a cab to take us to a check-cashing place. We rode around for more than an hour trying to find one that was open, and during that time he decided he wanted to be my friend? Look, I know I said that you have to put yourself out there socially, but this wasn't really what I meant. But still, my calm small talk may have saved my life.

"While we're here, tell me about yourself," I said. "Have you lived here your whole life? I just got here not more'n a few weeks ago and I'm havin' so much fun. . . . Are you interested in theatre?" I turned up my accent for extra charm. It worked: It literally disarmed him.

After we got my check cashed, he gave me back some of the money so I'd have enough to get by for the week. Then he told the cabdriver to take this long route back, and along the way he began pointing out the neighborhood where he was born, where he grew up . . . like he just wanted to show me around. Then he pushed me out of the cab and yelled, "Run, run, run!" so we wouldn't have to pay the poor driver. I ran because I didn't want to get shot.

Then the guy hugged me. "You're really cool. We should hang out sometime," he said.

"Well, you have to pay because I don't have any money left."

Then he disappeared and I never saw him again. I probably should have asked for his number.

Two days later, I was walking down into the subway station when a guy with a knife tried to rob me.

"You're too late. I was kidnapped and robbed two days ago."

"Oh. I'm sorry, I'm sorry," he said—and walked away.

I'd probably think this was bullshit if I was not the one this happened to, but I'm not even kidding you. The robber apologized to me.

I moved to a different neighborhood the next day and I never got robbed again, but I also didn't get any further in making my theatrical dreams come true. In the end, I worked myself into an actual mental breakdown and had to leave to get psychiatric help. I went back to Leesburg with my boyfriend, looking for comfort from my mom and grandparents, but I very quickly felt defeated—all the same reasons I left in the first place were still there, of course, and now I didn't even have the hope that I was going to break out and make it on Broadway.

Who knew that the perfect place for me was just an hour away from where I'd grown up?

Orlando was the "bad influence" they talked about in Leesburg.

"No one's happy there," my mother had told me. But it turned out to be the perfect mix: Life had been too slow in Leesburg and too fast in New York, but just like in the Goldilocks story, Orlando was just right. I found work there as a medical receptionist and then with the dinner theatres. I found out it was an absolute mecca of drag and of entertainers in general, many of whom worked at the theme parks. And slowly but surely, life got immeasurably better.

It wasn't the path I expected, but it was a great one anyway.

YES, AND . . .

In improv theatre, there's a practice known as "Yes, and." What it means, basically, is that you have to overcome your instinct to shut down whatever bizarreness has come your way, because if you don't accept the story line you're given it ruins the momentum and kills the rest of the scene.

So let's say you're doing a scene and the actor says, "Your dog just did a cartwheel!" You don't say, "I don't have a dog," or try to deflect and change the subject (that's a "No, but"). You say, "Yes, and she's working on her back handspring. She might have landed it, too, if that neighbor kid hadn't spooked her." You accept what the other person has said as the truth and then expand on it, moving the scene forward to where you think it should go next. In improv, you're in charge of not just reacting to things, but creating a doorway to the next thing.

This "Yes, and" attitude can also work in life. When you spend too much time "but"-ing yourself, you can talk yourself out of doing anything that involves a risk. Instead, no matter what craziness is happening to you or around you, figure out ways to accept the reality of your situation and then move it in the direction you want to go. Sometimes with improv, as in life, you can go too far into a harebrained scenario and realize you're never going to come to a reasonable conclusion (see: Grandpa and his chicken farm), but that's when it's time to yell, "Ta-daaa!," tap-dance away, and start a new scene!

Stay Open to the Unexpected

Throughout my career, I've played many of my dream roles. The first one that changed my life (well, after the Mayor of Munchkin City) was Hedwig in *Hedwig and the Angry Inch*. Which is funny, because I didn't even think I was going to accept the role. I'd recently seen the movie and didn't connect with the character—a feminine nonbinary person from Berlin who has a botched gender affirmation surgery because her crappy boyfriend insists on it (and then leaves Hedwig), and who's trying to become a rock star in America while also looking for real love. I said I didn't feel it was for me, and the producer said, "Forget the movie. Just read the words."

She gave me the script, and I was just a few pages into it when I started sobbing. I understood this person—who they were, where they came from, why people perceived them to be different. I felt for this person.

"I'll do it, as long as you allow me do it in a way that hasn't been done before. I don't want the same type of wig, the same costuming and voice . . . if you can give me the leeway to find this character in my own way, I want to do it," I said.

And to her credit, she did. I took physical inspiration from Divine and played the character in a way that I think was more warm and accessible than the movie . . . and more unhinged. It was supposed to be a three-week run at The Abbey in Orlando in 2012. It turned into two years.

In that time, I found myself in Hedwig. The character helped me to understand myself better as a nonbinary person and as a person struggling with bad relationships and a desire to be understood and accepted and loved for myself and for my talent. As my own life changed, the way I portrayed the character did, too. I went through my own stages of depression and mania and self-discovery as I also came to grips with my toxic relationship, and that colored my portrayal of Hedwig. It was an important time in my life and I was recognized well for it; lots of high-profile people saw the show, including RuPaul, and I think that was one of the reasons I was cast on *Drag Race* the following season.

My three favorite shows of all time are *Sweeney Todd*, *Little Shop of Horrors*, and *Gypsy*, all of which I think are expertly written. You can't cut a single line from them and have them make sense; everything is there for a reason. I've been lucky to be in all three of them.

STAGE FRIGHT

Sometimes people tell me that I seem so confident when I perform. "Don't you ever get stage fright?"

Yes, every performance, every time, and that's a good thing. Because when you stop having those butterflies, it means you've stopped caring and you should do something else.

Being nervous doesn't have to stop you from doing anything you want to do. It's an indication that you're invested in something and that you want to do it well. When you channel it, it adds to a performance because it gives you extra energy. For me, it's about self-talk and visualizations: I talk myself through what's going to happen.

"I'm stepping onto the stage; then I'm stepping to center stage where I'm in the spotlight. The show is going to be incredible. The jokes are just going to naturally land. When I do audience participation, we're all going to laugh together and have our shared experience. And then at the end of the day, I'm going to have a whole bunch of new fans and friends. I'm going to meet so many new people."

That's where I consciously direct my self-talk instead of letting myself play a loop of "I'm so nervous. What if it all goes wrong?" I reshape my nervousness into excitement by forcing myself to think about all the things that could go right.

Gypsy was an accident; I was costuming the show at the IceHouse Theatre in Mount Dora when the actress playing Mama Rose got into a knockdown fight with the director and quit two days before the show. I'd been there every night and I knew the show, so it was natural that I'd take over . . . except that I was a seventeen-year-old boy and had never really done drag before. But they were stuck, so they let me take over for a week while they trained a new actress, and that was a thrill. I was better than the new actress, by the way. (Sorry, new actress.)

I've always wanted a chance to play it again now, twenty years later, with more life experience and understanding behind me. It's still on my wish list.

The same kind of thing happened to me that same year with *Fiddler on the Roof*: I was directing the show when the guy playing Tevye called me before a matinee to say he had laryngitis. He could barely get out the words. I had one hour to pull myself together and play the role opposite a sixty-year-old Golde. Most of my "daughters" were older than I was. But that's part of the adventure and fun of theatre—getting to play roles no one expects you could play, so unlike yourself, with your adrenaline on overdrive because live shows are unpredictable.

It teaches you to stop boxing yourself in. I think actors get more exercise than most other people in learning to expand our definitions of who we are and what we can do, but that's a mindset anyone can adopt. So often, people get something stuck in their heads early in life, like "I'm not good at math" or "I'm a bad cook," and they might outgrow it and not even know it. All it takes is enough intention to change: to affirm for yourself that you're not "bad at" anything; you just need more practice.

Let Me Prove It to You

Another of my acting dreams came true when I was cast as Mrs. Lovett in *Sweeney Todd* at Clandestine Arts in Orlando, and we were just a couple weeks away from opening night when we got a cease and desist letter from Stephen Sondheim's representatives saying that he didn't want me in the role. Well, not me specifically (that would be hateful), but he didn't want any drag queen. They said the role had to be cast "honestly" as a woman. Stephen was not known for being agreeable (he called Lady Gaga's *Sound of Music* medley at the Oscars a "travesty"), but we decided to fight it. The company wrote back that we could submit a recording of me playing the role—all the songs, all the lines—during rehearsal for their consideration.

I'd just had knee surgery and wasn't even planning to do another rehearsal, but we now had less than a week to open and they were in danger of having to cancel the production or recast it at the last minute, so what choice was there? We emailed a recording and an hour later got a note back: "Stephen loves it." We were good to go, and I'd inadvertently auditioned for Stephen Sondheim.

It was gratifying to get reviews for that show like this one from *Orlando Weekly*: "Minj was much more than a gender-bending gimmick, putting aside her absurd eyelashes and Divine-worthy second-act outfit; she mined Lovett's mix of mercurial mania and girlish neediness much deeper than Helena Bonham Carter did in the movie, and

Ham It Up Hash

∽ 4 SERVINGS ∾

1 pound purple potatoes

½ cup apple cider vinegar

4 slices applewood smoked bacon, chopped

1 teaspoon salt

1½ teaspoons black pepper

½ cup chopped purple onion

1 large yellow bell pepper, seeded and diced

¼ cup chopped scallions

1. Put a large pot of water on to boil.

2. Wash and chop the potatoes into approximately 1-inch cubes. Place in a large bowl with the apple cider vinegar and allow to sit until the water is ready.

3. Once the water has reached a rolling boil, add the potatoes and vinegar. Allow to cook fully, about 15 minutes.

4. Cook the bacon in a large skillet or pan over medium heat.

5. When the potatoes are cooked, drain them and toss in the salt and pepper. Add the potatoes, onion, and bell pepper to the bacon and cook for approximately 5 minutes. Remove from the heat and toss with the scallions.

enunciated expertly in an accent to boot." Because that's the thing—I never wanted to be a gimmick, and I didn't see myself that way. I saw myself as an actor playing a part.

I love proving people wrong, and I appreciate producers and directors who take risks, rather than doing the same shows in the same costumes with people who look the same as the last time they did the show five years ago. I've always wanted a *Sound of Music* revival with Audra McDonald as Maria, and a *Mame* revival with Sheryl Lee Ralph in the title role. People get stuck on the past instead of envisioning what the future could be of these stories. And it's *meant* to be risky; every show is a fleeting moment in time just experienced by those people in that theatre, and if they come back the next night they should have a different experience. So why not push the boundaries and find out who plays these characters the best, regardless of what they look like?

Making Time for What You Love

Being on television is like sending out your audition tapes every week—it does a lot of advertising for you. Competing on *Drag Race* three times meant that I got a lot of invitations to do a lot of theatre, but I had to get pickier and pickier as time went on, because plays are usually months-long commitments, and because they usually pay like shit.

I make a lot more money doing drag than doing theatre, and it's tough to work around my schedule. But for the right role in the right show I still do it because I still love it and can't imagine my life without it. I think that's a key to happiness—you have to make the space for what lights your heart up.

I'd always wanted to perform Albin in *La Cage aux Folles*, for instance. *The Birdcage* was one of those movies I saw as a teen that helped me to see a flamboyantly gay, dramatic, over-the-top feminine-dressing man in a positive way, and *La Cage* is the musical version of it. When I was just eighteen, my community theatre was going to put on the show, but they got so much pushback from the town that they canceled it. That's one of the problems with living in the South: We're still behind on acceptance of positive portrayals of LGBTQIA+ people, even in theatre. I thought I had missed my chance forever.

Fifteen years later, I had a life-changing experience when I got to perform the *La Cage* song "I Am What I Am" in tribute to Harvey Fierstein at the Trailblazer Honors.

I was so nervous that I can't even remember the experience—it's like I blacked out when I walked out there and reassembled myself outside to have a cigarette afterward. Harvey wanted to meet me, and I had the gall to make that man come outside to see me because I needed the break.

"You don't know the weight of what you just did," he said. "What you gave to me and the world is something so beautiful it can never be re-created." That made me cry. Harvey was such a role model to me. I was twice cast to play Arnold in his play *Torch Song Trilogy*, which was a fantasy of mine because it was one of the movies I'd rented at the little gas station in Leesburg and hidden from my granny. I wrote to Harvey at the time to tell him how much it meant to me, and he wrote back with words of encouragement. He also wrote beautiful things when I was on season 7 of *Drag Race*.

Afterward, I got a lot of offers to play Albin, but theatres rarely had the budgets to do it right—and I don't want to spend my time working on shoestring productions that can't do the shows justice. That's not southern drama at all! We're all about being a little extra, not a little underwhelming.

CASTING STRAIGHT ACTORS

I had to consider whether or not it was hypocritical to object to straight actors playing gay roles, or cis people in trans roles—like the two straight guys in *Love, Simon* or James Corden in *The Prom*. After all, if what I just wrote is true, then doesn't that mean that anyone should be able to play any part they can act well?

This is what I came around to: LGBTQIA+ people have never been the first choice for roles. We've had to fight for the scraps—roles other people don't want, or roles that are demeaning. So I don't think it's a fair comparison; until we get to the point where we're not the bottom of the list even for parts that represent us, I think strong preference should be given to casting LGBTQIA+ people in LGBTQIA+ roles. Otherwise, showing allyship by telling our stories rings hollow.

In the end, producers mostly do whatever they think will draw a bigger audience, so if you want to be a good ally you can let them know on social media or otherwise that you'll show up for queer actors in queer roles.

Finally, I got the right offer from Music Theatre Works just outside of Chicago, which is where I am as of this writing, and we opened to rave reviews suggesting we should tour. So I guess I got to be a showgirl after all.

I've performed "I Am What I Am" twice more for Harvey Fierstein as part of promotional events for the show, and promised him the last time, "I swear I'm going to sing something else for you someday."

Imagine my delight, too, when fans started petitioning for me to play Ursula in the live-action remake of *The Little Mermaid*. The character's physicality was modeled after Divine, though she was never slated to play the role—the producers wanted Bea Arthur, but her agent turned it down. As far as I was concerned, I was the closest thing to Divine they were going to find. I'd even done a one-woman show at the Rochester FringeFestival called *Truly Divine*, an homage to her music and how she had influenced my life. And I'd performed and recorded "Poor Unfortunate Souls" before.

The Ursula thing turned into a viral movement; a bunch of *Drag Race* fans brought it up online, then they started actual online petitions, and then I woke up one day to all kinds of texts asking me: "Have you seen this??"—it was a *Billboard* article titled "Why Disney Should Cast Ginger Minj as Ursula in the Live-Action 'Little Mermaid' Remake."

What a thrill! It felt great to be recognized like this, and to have people fighting for me to play a role I so dearly wanted to play. All the attention did get me in the room; I don't think Disney was ever seriously considering casting me, but at least they now know who I am and I've done several projects with them since then. They even stepped slightly away from the safety zone and cast me to play the drag version of Bette Midler's character in *Hocus Pocus 2*.

The major barrier to casting me, or any other queen, is Disney's overseas distribution: Two of their biggest markets are in Russia and China, where it's illegal to show any kind of LGBTQIA+ content on film or television. Russia covers this under the "Gay Propaganda Law" of 2013, outlawing things like pride parades, which they say could influence minors to be sexual deviants. Casting me would have lost Disney the money from those markets, and they're not going to do that to take a stand. Disney has received mostly poor and failing marks from GLAAD's Studio Responsibility Index for this reason; they may have pride merchandise and high scores for their workplace

environment, but it's just starting to come through in respectful representation in their TV shows and movies.

But I'm not giving up. I love Disney and want them to keep making social progress. Disney World has always been a haven for LGBTQIA+ people—a blue oasis in the red sea of Florida—and I think it would be a big mistake for them to overlook our community's support. They had a misstep with their support of politicians who introduced the "Don't Say Gay" bill (it took me a lot of years to harness the power of the word "gay" and I'll be damned if some Eddie Munster–looking motherfucker is going to get me to stop saying it now) and they paid for it in the media.

I think there are still plenty of years and plenty of chances for me to play Ursula in the future, and it will stay with me that fans cared enough to fight for it. Hell, even people who don't particularly like me were on board. Thanks, losers.

And if you're wondering if I still have Broadway dreams, of course I do. Theatre kids are forever, and I am what I am.

9

What's Love Got to Do with It? My Obsession with Tina Turner

Tina Turner was the antithesis of everything I'd been told was beautiful. She was this older woman with spiky hair and scandalous miniskirts and she stomped around onstage singing in-your-face rock 'n' roll—and I was in love. She filled up the whole stage when she performed. She had this strength and power in the way she moved and sang, and I thought she was gorgeous. That's what I fell in love with before I knew anything about her story. But once I learned her background, I understood more where that strength came from . . . and I was _highly_ ticked off about it.

Nineteen ninety-three was the year I turned nine, the year _What's Love Got to Do with It_ was released, and also the year I cursed out Ike Turner.

Getting to that point required some subterfuge. Through a series of phone calls to the operator, I tracked down Ike's publicist's number. Then I called and earnestly explained that I was Ike's biggest fan and that my life's dream was to talk to him on the phone.

"I just think he's the best. He wrote the first rock 'n' roll song and he didn't even get credit for it! That is just wrong."

Now, some of that was true—I did think Ike was a talented musician. But that had nothing to do with why I was calling. Using my father's brand of southern charm, I'd employed compliments and conversation to get from one person to another on the phone until I gained an audience with my nemesis to unleash the appropriate level of adolescent wrath.

"Mr. Turner, I just want to tell you one thing: You're a nasty motherfucker and I can't believe you beat Tina! I hate you! I fucking hate you!"

Kids don't have any sense of time. Ike hadn't seen Tina in close to twenty years, but since I'd just learned about it, it felt highly relevant. I was in the middle of a rage stroke when my father heard me screaming at someone and walked into the room.

"Who are you talking to?"

"Ike Turner!"

"What??"

He grabbed the phone out of my hand and spoke into it. "Who is this?"

"Ike Turner. Who the fuck is this?"

My father hung up and I was grounded for about a year and a half, but it was worth it. I had fulfilled my quest to stand up for the great and powerful diva who was my first true passion: Tina Turner. Now, it's probably not all that common for a nine-year-old boy to have an unrelenting obsession with Tina Turner, but you already know I was not a very common kid.

There's nobody in the world who sounds like Tina Turner, because she doesn't sing like a trained singer. She gets to the notes in her own way. She's also not a trained dancer; she stomps and gyrates the way she feels, not in a choreographed way. That's why it's been so spectacularly hard to cast the Broadway musical about her—who can do Tina except Tina?

I loved to imitate her when I sang. But my love for her grew exponentially after I saw the movie about her life *What's Love Got to Do with It?* and read her memoir *I, Tina*.

She was a country bumpkin—born Anna Mae Bullock in Nutbush, Tennessee—whose family didn't have any money, and who had a chaotic and violent household like my own. They were sharecroppers, and everyone worked in the cotton field. Her main

Not-So-Fancy Fried Spam

4 SERVINGS

Tina's chef, Dez Harkness, was amazed by one of Tina's requests on tour: Spam! She said it was a "wonderful type of meat" she "had as a child." Who am I to argue?

1 can Spam

3 tablespoons soy sauce

2 tablespoons pineapple juice

2 tablespoons maple syrup

1 tablespoon minced garlic

1 teaspoon onion powder

2 teaspoons black pepper

Vegetable oil to coat bottom of pan

Scallions (for topping, optional)

1. Start by cutting your Spam into ½-inch slices and placing them on a baking sheet. In a small bowl, whisk together the soy sauce, pineapple juice, maple syrup, garlic, onion powder, and pepper and pour generously over your sliced meat. Cover and allow to refrigerate overnight.

2. Heat some oil in a frying pan over medium heat and drop your Spam slices in three at a time, being careful not to overcrowd the pan. As the slices fry, use the leftover glaze to baste the tops. Flip your slices until they are crispy and golden all over. Repeat with the remaining slices and serve with a side of rice. And don't be afraid to gussy it up with some scallions!

joy at the time was singing in the church choir at the little Baptist church, because there was nothing else to do. Her idea of cuisine was the kind of canned food you get at food pantries.

Tina's mother abandoned the family when Tina was eleven, and then her father left right after that, too, which maybe didn't come as a shock. Tina had already felt unwanted and unloved. She and her sisters stayed with a cousin and Tina kept hoping her mother would come back for them, but she didn't. Then Tina was separated from her siblings and moved in with her grandparents. In her teens she worked as a maid. Eventually her grandmother died and Tina moved back in with her mother until she finished high school. She worked as a nurse's aide after graduation.

But you know what? This little girl who felt unloved and different and poor and not pretty grew up to be the fucking queen of rock 'n' roll. And that inspired the hell out of me, as it should anyone—it teaches us to never believe that we're stuck where we were planted. We can love ourselves enough to make up for the lack of love others have shown us.

It's easy to forget that Tina Turner was ever . . . *not* Tina Turner. Her presence is enormous, and she's been an icon for more than forty years. People know she escaped Ike's abuse, but they don't usually talk about the adversity she overcame before she ever met Ike. Adversity that I felt a kinship with, even before my life took a series of turns that closely matched with hers. Plus, we looked exactly alike.

"I want to be a star like that," I thought. "When you can stand tall and sing and wear beautiful golden dresses, people like you. They scream your name." That's what I imagined . . . feeling liked and wanted by thousands—no, millions!—of strangers who would show up and cheer for me.

Becoming a singer like Tina didn't seem entirely out of the question some days. Parts of me believed I had talent. Parts of me thought I was interesting and funny. Then there was the part of me that thought I'd be better off dead. Tina did the same thing—she attempted suicide by overdosing on sleeping pills, thinking she was in an inescapably bad situation. She felt worthless aside from her singing.

First my feelings of worthlessness were implanted in me by my father and other family members, and then, as I got older, they were reinforced by the men I dated.

As my life marched on, I found myself having more and more in common with Tina, not always in a good way. Dating abusive assholes was my specialty. Tina was seventeen when she met twenty-five-year-old Ike at a nightclub in St. Louis with her older sister, who used to sneak her in. He was there performing with his band, Kings of Rhythm. She wasn't attracted to him (she ended up dating the band's saxophonist instead), but she was mesmerized by his guitar playing. She kept coming back to watch the band, and asking him to let her sing with them. He politely blew her off, but one day the drummer dropped the mic in front of her, so she took her opportunity—she sang with the band and stole the show. Because she is Tina Freaking Turner.

Well, Ike knew a meal ticket when he saw it. He first invited her to be a backup singer, and then his co-lead singer when it became clear audiences were there to see her. He gave her the stage name Tina Turner even though they weren't married until years later—he just wanted people to think they were. Then he trademarked the name so that if they ever split up he could hire another singer and call her Tina Turner. He treated her like his property, like she was supposed to be so thankful he "discovered" her that she would overlook all the physical and mental abuse he was piling on her.

My relationships often worked the same way.

My first real boyfriend and I met online before that was a common thing; I was fifteen and he was close to thirty, and at first it made me feel special to have his attention.

YOUR BIGGER LIFE

The main thing I took from Tina was the inspiration to dream bigger. It's very easy to box yourself into the same type of life your family lived, or the same level of education or income of the people around you. When you grow up without much, you can start thinking that's your limit.

But you can design your life just like little kids draw pictures: colorful and big and full of imagination and joy. When Tina was this unwanted teenager working minimum-wage jobs, she had to step back from her day-to-day "getting by" mindset to draw herself a bigger picture, and then follow through with those leaps of faith it took to get there. She decided she was going to be a singer, and she put herself into situations where she could show off her talent even when no one was asking for it. She didn't wait for invitations, applications, or certifications. You don't have limits either.

Bigger doesn't have to mean New York City or LA either, like I originally thought. You can live in the South and be a star. Lots of celebrities do: Reese Witherspoon, Usher, Justin Timberlake, Zach Galifianakis, Mary Steenburgen and Ted Danson, Serena Williams. . . . I find it doesn't matter much where you choose to live as long as you stay near a decent airport. If you're planning to be a big ole superstar like me, then sure, you'll have to travel, but you can do it. Think of all the free little toiletries you can swipe from hotels.

I thought he was handsome and mature . . . he, too, thought he was handsome and mature. He took advantage of me sexually and broke me down so that I felt he was doing me a favor by being willing to date a little fat teenager like me.

It set me up to think this was a normal relationship—I'd had such little experience with what love was supposed to look like, and I definitely had "daddy issues." I just wanted a man to love me. I didn't know any gay boys my own age, and even if I did, I probably wouldn't have related to them—I was already basically on my own after I dropped out of school. I stayed with my grandparents most of the time but also couch-surfed at friends' houses. I made my own money and took care of myself as best I could, so it made me feel good that an adult was taking me seriously as someone to date. Even when he told me that I was so *lucky* he was dating me, because no one else would want me.

We dated for years, and it chipped away at my self-worth even more. I didn't learn my lesson from it, though, and when I arrived in New York the same thing happened all over again. Another older man with a bad temper who constantly reminded me that I wasn't really good enough for him.

He told me I was ugly, that I was fat. When I had my breakdown in New York, he came with me back to Florida, but he was miserable about it and never let me forget it. It was a constant barrage of guilt, reminding me that I took him away from his life and moved him to this backwards place.

"I gave up my entire life for you! I sacrificed everything," he'd say.

He couldn't hold down a job; he'd work sporadically and get fired, so I was paying our bills. It was up to me to make sure we had a car, to pay the rent, all of it. After a while, I was doing drag shows nearly every night, wherever I could find the work, to supplement my other jobs. All small stuff: fifty dollars here, one hundred dollars there, but it got us through.

He said I was sacrificing my appearance to drag—which was partly true. It was easier for me to have long fingernails and shave my eyebrows and grow long hair so I wouldn't have to work as hard at my makeup and fake nails.

"I'm not attracted to women," he said. Yet he also reminded me that I wasn't attractive as a boy, so it felt like damned if I do, damned if I don't.

I was so passive about it, not wanting to do anything to anger him. I did feel beholden to him because he'd moved for me—I felt so bad that he was unhappy there, but I couldn't go back to New York. My mental health wouldn't allow it. What I'd learned from that experience was that I wasn't meant for big-city life, even if that's what I had once dreamed about. It was all just too overwhelming, too much. I love excitement and shows, but I also need my quiet time—and there's practically no such thing in New York City. It's like living in the middle of a fucking parade all the time.

So I tried to do like Granny taught me to keep my man happy. I worked hard and I cooked and I tried to make ours a good home, in the hopes that he would come around and decide that I was enough and this place was enough. It was exhausting trying to heal my own mental health while also caring for someone who was so filled with negativity about me and everything around us. But I swear I tried.

Finding Clarity

Just like Tina knew Ike was cheating on her, I knew my man was running around on me, which I also sort of accepted out of a sense of guilt. I had such little self-esteem left. The only thing I still felt good about was my talent; I knew I was a good performer, and that I could dress up in women's clothes and make myself pretty and entertain people. But I didn't feel good about Joshua. I felt worthless, unsexy, unattractive, unlovable. This went on for more than a decade.

In the HBO documentary *Tina*, she says she tried so hard to forget Anna Mae Bullock existed. She felt that the goodness in her life did not balance out the bad, and she wanted to leave the past behind. But at the same time, Tina was a persona—wigs and makeup and performing with a smile even when that was totally fake because everything was upside down offstage. So she had to reconcile the two pieces of herself.

When Kurt Loder was interviewing her for her first book in 1985, he asked about whether she'd given up love for the sake of her career. "I have not received love almost ever in my life. I did not have it with my mother or father from the beginning of birth and I survived. Why did I get so far without love?" she asked. "I have had not one love affair that was genuine and sustained itself. Not one. Kurt, I've been through fucking tons of heartbreak. I've analyzed it. I've said, 'What's wrong with me?' I've looked in the mirror with myself stripped of makeup and without hair. Why can't someone see the beauty in the woman it is that I am?"

I felt that *hard*. She stuck with Ike for sixteen years, not telling anyone what was happening. There's a thing that's pretty common in relationship abuse: The person who's being abused doesn't see it for what it is, even if any reasonable outsider would. You can get into the slow descent from the happy honeymoon stage into the first signs of trouble and think, "He didn't mean to do that. He's never done that before. I must have done something to set him off." Or, "It's just because he drank too much." And then once you accept it a couple times, it just becomes part of the fabric of your relationship and you forget you never agreed to this and just because you put up with it once doesn't mean you have to again. You start feeling like it's your problem to solve. The rules have changed.

For me, it was years and years of believing the abuse was in some way my fault. I was ugly, I was weak, and this man was out of my league. I was really just starting to see it for what it was after eleven years together. He was so controlling, and when the emotional abuse wasn't working on me anymore that's when the physical abuse ramped up.

Then I came home a day early after filming *Drag Race*, and walked in on him having sex with his best friend in my house.

You'd think I would be the one to lose my shit here, but what actually happened was that I said, "You know what? You can have him. I'm done. I don't want to be a part of this anymore." And then he got really, really mad and followed me out of the room and started punching me.

I had the oddest reaction: I just started laughing.

I laughed because in that moment the thought that came to mind was this: "You wanted to be like Tina Turner. Well, you've never been more like Tina than at this moment."

It was my moment of clarity, like watching my life play out on a screen in front of me. I'd seen Tina's movie. I'd read the book. I knew the blueprint of this; this was abuse, and it was time for me to get out.

I took the heeled shoe out of my bag and hit him in the face with it, and I said, "You're never going to touch me again."

He was stunned; I'd never fought back before. But I was done. I walked away for good at that moment, and started rebuilding my relationship with myself. Just like Tina did.

The Big Mock

4 BURGERS

The other thing Tina requested on tour was hamburgers, which her chef served on Big Mac buns.

FOR THE SPECIAL SAUCE

4 tablespoons ketchup

3 tablespoons mayonnaise

1 tablespoon sweet relish

FOR THE BURGERS

1 pound lean ground beef

1 tablespoon black pepper

1 teaspoon salt

½ teaspoon onion powder

½ teaspoon garlic powder

1 teaspoon crushed garlic

¼ teaspoon dill

8 hamburger buns with sesame seeds

Dill pickles

Shredded lettuce

16 slices American cheese

1. Start by whisking your ketchup, mayonnaise, and relish together in a small bowl. Refrigerate until needed.

2. In a large mixing bowl, combine the ground beef, pepper, salt, onion powder, garlic powder, crushed garlic, and dill. Mix well by hand until all the ingredients come together. Be careful not to overmix, because you don't want tough patties!

3. Use an ice-cream scoop to drop your meat mixture into a sizzling pan. As your patties begin to cook, use a spatula to flatten them. You'll want thin, crispy patties for best results here.

4. Generously dollop your special sauce on the tops and bottoms of the buns and spread into an even layer, being careful not to get too close to the edges. Add the pickles and shredded lettuce to the top bun and begin stacking your patties: one on the bottom bun topped by a slice of cheese, then another on top of that crowned with another slice of cheese. Carefully place the top and serve with your favorite French fries or onion rings!

Moving On and Moving Up

"I am worthy." That's what I had to keep telling myself after I left. It was like removing layers and layers of hate from my skin so I could start to see what I was underneath. My whole life, men who were supposed to love me had knocked me down with insults and judgments, and I had to retrain myself not to believe them anymore.

Like so many other abusers, my ex was charming and able to fool a lot of people, convincing them that I had left him with nothing. For two years, someone claiming to be one of his friends kept posting the same story on social media, saying that I'd taken everything including the bed and he had to start a GoFundMe to afford rent. Every time I blocked him, he popped up again under a different name. I had to walk away from defending myself because it wasn't where I wanted to spend my energy; I just wanted to close that chapter of my life for good, and whoever wanted to believe him could do that. The truth is that many of them came around and eventually realized how toxic he was, but by then it was a big ole whatever for me.

Tina hated Ike for many years but eventually found that to be a wasted emotion. Even though reporters have asked her about him every interview for decades and decades after they split up, she never really wanted to talk about him after it was over. She wanted to tell her story once so people understood what happened, and then she wanted to close the door on it and live her life without that trauma always casting a shadow on her future. I took a lesson from that, too.

It's not that you never think about it again, or that you can never feel down about it, but the important thing is to analyze why it happened—figure out how you got into an abusive relationship and why you stayed after the first signs, and then make the real decision in your heart that that will never happen to you again because you will love yourself so much that no one will be able to take that away from you.

That part was hard. When you grow up with criticism hitting you from all angles, it takes over your inner voice. I had to consciously work at respecting myself.

Tina found love again with a wonderful man and completely reinvented her spirituality. She found an inner clarity through Buddhism, and what I took away from her explanations of the religion was that you should be open and loving and empathetic to

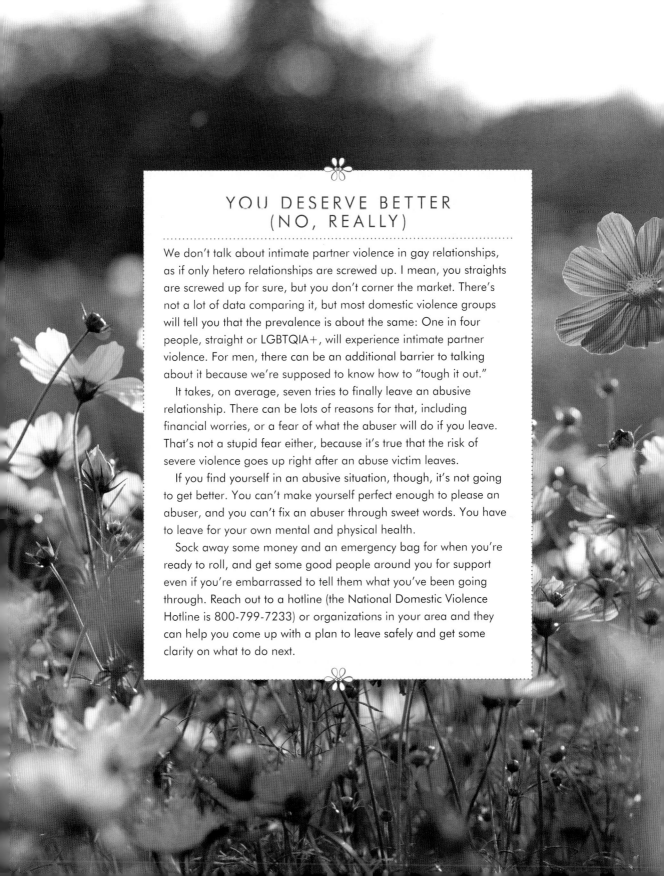

YOU DESERVE BETTER
(NO, REALLY)

We don't talk about intimate partner violence in gay relationships, as if only hetero relationships are screwed up. I mean, you straights are screwed up for sure, but you don't corner the market. There's not a lot of data comparing it, but most domestic violence groups will tell you that the prevalence is about the same: One in four people, straight or LGBTQIA+, will experience intimate partner violence. For men, there can be an additional barrier to talking about it because we're supposed to know how to "tough it out."

It takes, on average, seven tries to finally leave an abusive relationship. There can be lots of reasons for that, including financial worries, or a fear of what the abuser will do if you leave. That's not a stupid fear either, because it's true that the risk of severe violence goes up right after an abuse victim leaves.

If you find yourself in an abusive situation, though, it's not going to get better. You can't make yourself perfect enough to please an abuser, and you can't fix an abuser through sweet words. You have to leave for your own mental and physical health.

Sock away some money and an emergency bag for when you're ready to roll, and get some good people around you for support even if you're embarrassed to tell them what you've been going through. Reach out to a hotline (the National Domestic Violence Hotline is 800-799-7233) or organizations in your area and they can help you come up with a plan to leave safely and get some clarity on what to do next.

everybody, but you shouldn't let any of that get in the way of your inner peace and your vision for your life.

She was able to fully move on and feel like that dark part of her life was far behind her, so I took that as a goal, too. I wanted to believe that I could find real happiness in a relationship someday, and that I could learn to value myself enough not to ever put up with abuse again.

I didn't really feel hatred toward any of my exes; I don't live in a place of bitterness, because that shit can eat you alive. The southern way is to wish people well and keep your dignity intact and bless their stupid hearts, which is what I've tried to do.

While I was touring in Vegas this year, a mutual friend of ours contacted me to let me know that my ex had passed away, presumably of heart disease. Then suddenly I was getting tagged in all sorts of tributes to him online, which hurt because it felt like he'd been a great guy to everyone but me . . . why me? It momentarily brought me back to a place where I wondered, "What was wrong with me that I triggered his abuse?" But that's never the right question. The only real question is: "Why did I believe I deserved that kind of hate and how can I love myself better so I never fall into that again?"

People have a tendency to saint the dead, and I don't want to do that. I believe he died as a better person than he was when we were together, and I'm glad for that. I wish I had known that person.

Abuse can brainwash you. When you've been through it, you have to reteach yourself about your worth and about what a healthy relationship should be. I highly recommend finding a good therapist to help with this, but at the very least, start journaling and writing down all the positive things you can think of about yourself. Remind yourself every day that you are a lovable and good person, and that you don't need to settle for someone dysfunctional again.

This is what I want you to replay in your mind:

* "I have nothing to feel ashamed or bad about."

* "I didn't cause this."

* "I didn't deserve it."

* "I am worthy of love."

* "Life will get better."

* "I have a great ass."

* "Ginger Minj really should play Ursula someday."

When you're ready, you should also ask your friends to stop talking about your ex. I found it helpful to set the boundary—I didn't need to hear anything good *or* bad about him anymore. I didn't need affirmation of how terrible he was to me and how glad they were I was away from him. I just needed him to be out of my headspace entirely. I would never get the kind of closure I originally hoped for—an apology—but one day like the little Disney princess I am, I went outside and talked to the moon and had this great feeling come over me: *You're doing fine.*

So find your way out, and walk away for good. Then go put on a miniskirt, stomp around your living room, and remember you're Simply the Best. Better than all the rest.

....

German Brown Bread

∽ 1 LOAF ∽

Tina has said she maintains her figure by eating bananas, kiwi, melon, and traditional German brown bread every single morning, and that really struck a chord with me because I, too, maintain my figure by eating bread. Lots and lots of bread. I have to admit, it wasn't until I was older and out of Lake County that I even discovered what German brown bread was, but now it's my favorite. Maybe because of Tina, or maybe just because it pairs so well with literally everything. I love it with soup, I love it as French toast, and my favorite is pan-toasting it with some sliced turkey, cranberry chutney, thin sliced apples, and cream cheese for the most delicious sandwich you could imagine!

I've combined my favorite pieces of a few different recipes over the years to create what I believe to be the most versatile bread in the world. NOTE: You will need a sourdough starter for this recipe. I'll include a basic recipe for that as well, but you can use any sourdough starter.

FOR THE SOURDOUGH
STARTER

**2 cups warm water
(plus ½ cup for day 5)**

**1 packet (¼ ounce) active
dry yeast**

**2 cups all-purpose flour
(plus 1 cup for day 5)**

FOR THE GERMAN
BROWN BREAD

3 cups all-purpose flour

2 cups wheat flour

½ cup rolled oats

2 teaspoons salt

2 teaspoons caraway seeds

1 teaspoon brown sugar

**1½ teaspoons instant
dry yeast**

1 cup buttermilk

1 cup plain yogurt

1 tablespoon vinegar

¼ cup sourdough starter

1 tablespoon vegetable oil

2 cups water

1 spray bottle of water

MAKE THE SOURDOUGH STARTER

1. Place the 2 cups warm water and the yeast in a medium bowl and mix until fully dissolved. Slowly stir in the 2 cups flour, mixing until all lumps are gone and the mixture is smooth. Make sure your starter takes up only about half the space of your container so that it has space to grow.

2. Cover your container with a cloth or towel, securing in place with a rubber band. Place in the refrigerator for 5 days, stirring daily.

3. On day 5, feed your starter by removing half of it from the container (you can use this for your first batch of bread!), adding the 1 cup flour and the ½ cup warm water and allowing to sit for 1 hour before returning to the fridge.

MAKE THE GERMAN BROWN BREAD

1. In a large bowl, mix together the flours, oats, salt, caraway seeds, brown sugar, and yeast.

2. In a small bowl, mix together your buttermilk, yogurt, and vinegar.

3. Add the wet mixture and sourdough starter to your dry ingredients and mix together with a large spoon until the ingredients are well blended and the dough has formed a ball. The texture should be slightly sticky, so feel free to add 1 to 2 tablespoons of warm water as needed when mixing.

4. Drop your dough onto a lightly floured surface and knead for 5 minutes, allow to sit for 5 minutes, then knead for another 2. Re-form into a ball.

5. Grease your large bowl with the oil, then drop the dough in, turning to make sure the top is well coated.

6. Cover the bowl with a kitchen towel and place in a warm area to rise until your dough has doubled in size.

7. Place a baking dish with 2 cups of water on the bottom rack of your oven and preheat to 500°F.

8. Mold your bread into the desired shape, place on a lined baking sheet, and dust generously with flour. Allow to rise until the loaf has doubled in size.

9. About 30 minutes before baking, score the top of your bread at least ¼ inch deep.

10. Place your baking sheet on the center rack and allow to bake for 10 minutes, spraying the sides of the oven with water after 3, 6, and 9 minutes.

11. Turn the temperature down to 450°F and bake for 15 minutes.

12. Reduce the temperature to 350°F and bake for 25 to 30 minutes, until the loaf is golden brown and sounds hollow when tapped.

13. Remove from the oven and allow to cool for at least 2 hours before slicing and serving.

10
Drag Pageants

·············· ❦ ··············

For most of America, the first real education they got about drag was from RuPaul and other TV and movie stars. And when *Drag Race* came along, no one—*no one*—expected it to be the giant mainstream hit that it is. But giving people an opportunity to see drag from the safety of their living rooms made them realize how much fun it is, and how it's not just a dirty, overly sexual, gay-man niche thing—which they may have believed based on garbage talk shows in the nineties that loved to start fights and make fools of drag queens.

RuPaul had a lot to overcome when starting a show to celebrate drag. So many people thought of it as a freak show, and she made people see it in a totally different light: It was about celebrating over-the-top feminine style and manner.

Another thing I think is so appealing about *Drag Race* is that it's so multifaceted. You have to be a great designer to go on *Project Runway*, but you don't have to be able to wear those clothes, paint your face, sing a song, choreograph a dance, and film a little movie based around it all at the same time. On other reality competition shows, you have to be good at one thing, but drag queens are self-taught to be good at everything.

And people are finally starting to see that now we're becoming the ones who push fashion forward. Things you see on *Drag Race* last season are inspiring designer collections on the runway the following year. Not only that, but you've got queens from our show walking in the Fenty fashion shows and modeling for them online also. It's changing the way mainstream America deals with gender. You can have somebody of any gender who happens to look beautiful in an outfit walk down the runway and model it, which allows more people to see representation of themselves.

Plus-size fashion has also undergone a major transformation that I think is influenced by drag. When I used to go to Ross fifteen years ago, the women's plus-size collections were all so drab. Browns and grays, everything meant to make us look smaller and less noticeable. Nowadays you're just as likely to find bright colors and pom-poms and fringe. You can't tell me that drag queens didn't have a place in helping push body acceptance forward. I believe that the more people saw queens on their TV strutting their stuff in outrageous outfits and makeup, the more women started seeing that they could take bigger risks with their choices, too, and not look like idiots. If they believed we looked beautiful, then surely they could, too.

How Drag Got Its Start

Throughout the 1900s, drag was this niche thing that was mostly for the LGBTQIA+ population, tucked away (see what I did there?) in gay clubs and bars, with occasional vaudeville-esque performances for the straights, mostly as comic relief.

Pageants were the way to make a name for yourself and become a celebrity in the drag world. If you wanted to make money as a drag performer, you had to convince clubs to book you and pay you—not just let you work for tips—and that meant they had to believe you were someone special who could draw an audience. The big pageants themselves also offered guaranteed paid bookings throughout the year.

The earliest recorded drag pageants came from the drag balls in Harlem in the late 1800s and early 1900s, where "costume contests" were part of the activities. Then the young queen Flawless Sabrina began hosting separate drag pageants throughout the country in 1959—even though cross-dressing was illegal and she kept getting arrested (at least one hundred times, she estimated). Her 1967 Miss All-America Camp Beauty Pageant was the setting for the classic drag pageant documentary *The Queen*, where Crystal LaBeija loudly protested the judge's decision ("I have a *right* to show my color, darling. I'm beautiful and I know I'm beautiful!") because it was nearly impossible for queens of color to win pageants. Crystal then founded the House of LaBeija in 1972 and became a mother figure to homeless LGBTQIA+ youth.

Then came the big national pageants that still exist today, starting with Miss Gay America in 1972. Miss Gay America doesn't allow contestants with any kind of body enhancements—no hormones, no surgeries from the neck down. So it excluded most trans women, which I think is silly, and that's why other pageants such as Miss Continental and Miss USofA were launched, to be more inclusive. But then that skewed in the opposite direction: For the first several years, it was really hard to win Miss Continental if you *weren't* trans.

You can find all kinds of drag pageants—besides the really big ones, there are also regional and themed ones. Lots of *Drag Race* girls have won or placed in some of the big pageants (Alyssa Edwards, Kennedy Davenport, Coco Montrese, Alexis Mateo, Trinity K. Bonet, Asia O'Hara, Naysha Lopez . . .). I got into it, though, because of Carmella Marcella Garcia.

THE OLD RULES

Etiquette rules in pageants can be really over-the-top and outdated—for Miss Gay America, you can't drink, smoke, or swear; you have to dress and act a certain way . . . for a *drag pageant*. It doesn't make any sense to me. It doesn't celebrate who we are. Instead, it makes me think of when my family would tell me, "You need to be normal." Miss Gay America should be the symbol of excellence and the leader for our entire community, the way we really are: uncensored, risqué, norm-defying people who speak our minds. Why should she try to conform and be what a "real" Miss America is? (Which has always been pretty phony anyway.)

I truly want drag pageants to thrive well into the future, but to draw back the kinds of popularity they had before they need to get with the times and let us do what we do best.

So much is supposed to evolve with the times, whether that's technology or our understanding of ourselves and other people. You may come to a point where you realize the life you've created for yourself was based on outdated rules. You may still be operating under ideas you held when you were a kid—things you were taught once upon a time that no longer need to apply to you. Consider modernizing your mind every now and then: taking stock of what you believe spiritually, politically, socially . . . making sure that your life is in alignment with your true self and not an authority figure's old rules.

The first time I saw her was when I was a baby queen and she was hosting the regional preliminary Miss Continental pageant I went to see. I just fell in love with her. I loved the way she handled an audience. She would be canceled today for half the things she said, because she was not politically correct at *all*. But that's where drag was. I think that while it's important to hold people accountable, especially when they're given a platform like *Drag Race* that's worldwide and speaks to so many people, it's also really, really important to remember that drag became popular by taking all these social norms and turning them on their head. It was always leading the conversation to bring about change.

I found out that Carmella was the national host for Miss Continental, which meant that she got to travel around to any of the prelims that she wanted to. They would fly her there, put her up, pay for her meals, and pay her to host their pageants. And then she went on and hosted the four-day national pageant every year.

"That would be the sweetest gig," I thought. You would always know where your check was coming from, exactly how many bookings you were going to have throughout the year, and what you could rely on. And you got to be the head of the biggest, most glamorous drag stage. *I want to do that!*

Then I found out the only reason she got that gig was because she was a former Miss Continental. (Not only that, but she'd won darn near every national pageant also, and rightfully so. After she retired from pageants, she became a coach for the actual Miss America pageant.) So I said, "Oh, so now I have to win the pageant so I can become the national host." That's what drove me to do it.

Carmella's humor appeared effortless. She was just a very quick-witted person. But I never understood until I sat and talked with her in the dressing rooms what a hard worker she was—to see how much she planned and refined every joke. Every piece of hair, every costume, nothing was thrown together. Everything was thought out.

Even when she was funny, she was very serious about it because this was her job, her art, and her craft and something she'd dedicated her entire life to.

That's something I found hopeful: We can sometimes believe that other people have it *so easy*—that they're just naturally good at things and we're not. But she reminded me that even "naturals" are usually people who've out-practiced everyone else.

Which goes back to the very southern habit of:

"Girl, I love your dress!"

"This old thing? Oh, I just had it in the back of my closet."

Bitch, you did *not*. You had that thing steamed and pressed and accessorized and altered and shoes dyed to match just so you could flutter your eyes and pretend. That's what Carmella did with comedy.

And she opened my eyes about what a pageant girl could look like. I would never have thought of myself as a beauty queen, but because she did, it gave me permission to. Pageantry is something more than a "drag competition." Competition is just about fighting for the crown, but pageantry is a show that welcomes people in. I think it's an important distinction, even though everyone obviously wants to win. It's culturally so significant to the gay community and such a big piece of drag history from the not-so-distant past when drag was much more taboo.

It gave girls a place to dress up and perform and meet other queens and feel less alone, because many of us had been through the same kinds of trauma: family rejection, bullying, being socially outcast, church abuse . . . and lots of the same kinds of results: self-harm, drug and alcohol abuse, depression, anxiety, shame. There was value in coming together and deciding that we were all beautiful, talented people. (Except that one bitch who tried to steal your man, of course.)

If you wanted to travel, competing in pageants was the way to accomplish that. The thing is, there's very little money to be made from most prizes because you spend so much getting to that point. For nationals, you need at least two gowns for preliminaries and finals, with your second gown being better than your first (the first one has to be good enough to get you to the finals, but the second has to *win*). Then you need your interview suit, makeup, and wigs, and also your travel and hotel and meals, payment for your backup dancers for your talent acts (at least two acts), tickets for your backup dancers to get in (usually $75 each), so you can easily wind up spending $15,000–$20,000 and needing to take a full week off work.

I was showing up with $10,000 worth of stuff and being made fun of because it wasn't good enough. And you're doing all that for the chance of being the one person who'll win $4,000 and your booking fees.

But the value isn't in the prize money; it's in what it could do for the rest of your career. I used it to build up my charisma, uniqueness, nerve, and talent. It helps you learn how to handle interview questions, and not just to speak articulately into a microphone, but to speak authentically and passionately. And if you want honest feedback, a friend backstage at a pageant will deliver: "Do I look all right?" "No, bitch, you look busted. Why would you wear that?" There's no time for politeness; pageants move fast.

If you got a title, from then on you had something to put after your name in your promotions. You were no longer "Deva Station from Ohio"; now you were "Deva Station, Miss Gay America."

Contest wins and titles can give you confidence, something to put on a résumé, and something to embroider on your jacket so Cindy Lou Who can choke on her gum when she sees you at the grocery store.

Jimmy's Chicken Salad

⌒ 6 SERVINGS ⌒

Jimmy was my first promoter, the one who told me to enter Miss Continental Plus. Every year, it was on Easter weekend and it felt like a family reunion to see people we saw only once a year. Jimmy would get the biggest suite at the Conrad Hotel and cook for everyone, with my help. His chicken salad was the big hit, and everyone at the pageant would make their way into his room on Easter Sunday before the show and make themselves a platter.

His secret ingredient was ground ginger, and he told me that if I disappointed him at the pageant he was going to get it fresh.

4 chicken breasts

**4 tablespoons honey
(plus more for basting)**

1 cup orange juice

¾ cup mayonnaise

2 celery stalks, finely chopped

1 teaspoon grated garlic

1 tablespoon black pepper

½ tablespoon salt

1 tablespoon ground ginger

1 tomato, sliced

Bibb lettuce

1. Marinate the chicken breasts overnight in a mixture of honey and orange juice.

2. Preheat the oven to 400°F.

3. Drain the mixture and bake the chicken for 25 minutes, or until the internal temperature reaches 165°F, basting with honey as you go. The chicken should be caramelized and delicious when you're done! Set it aside until it's cool enough to shred. Set the shredded chicken aside in a medium mixing bowl.

4. Add the mayonnaise, celery, garlic, pepper, salt, and ginger to the chicken. Mix thoroughly. Cover the bowl and refrigerate for 20 minutes.

5. Sandwich a generous helping between two thick-cut slices of toast with as much tomato and Bibb lettuce as you please and enjoy!

Competing for a Crown

My first pageant was Miss Gay Days 2008, part of a huge weeklong event centered around Disney World. I went into it with a borrowed gown and second-rate makeup, and I won first alternate (second place), with Coco Montrese winning the crown. My very first pageant! They were forgiving of my subpar appearance because I got a perfect score on my Q&A and my talent act: a very theatrical, twisted, sensational *Wizard of Oz* act where Dorothy ends up getting electroshock therapy in the loony bin. Most of the other contestants were lip-synching for their acts, so mine stood out.

It gave me the confidence to believe I could do well in the pageant world, so from there I was all in. I immediately entered the next local pageant I could find: Miss Twisters of Central Florida, about an hour away from Orlando in this little bar in Polk County. I got there and it looked like a double-wide trailer. If you google it now, you'll find no trace of it except in my bio, but that's okay, because I won the darn thing and it helped boost my standing in the Orlando community a lot. I had a crown! That meant I got more bookings.

My life was crazy at that time because I was working so many jobs at once. I'd start the morning doing my costume and wig work at Sleuths, then in the afternoon I'd do a children's show for school groups, then a quick break to get into drag for the dinner shows at Sleuths (sometimes two in a row), and finally I'd work at a nightclub—which might be down the road, or might be three hours away. Then I'd get home and have to get out of drag and do it all over again the next day. I can't imagine that kind of schedule now, but it was fun then, and I was so appreciative of all of it. It finally felt like I was doing what I was meant to do.

I got really obsessed with analyzing drag pageants. I bought tickets to see them all around the South when I wasn't in them. I knew who the contestants were, how they did in each category, what the point breakdowns were, how to maximize your points. . . . I went into it strategically, knowing that every win, and particularly a big national win, would raise my profile much further.

It helped to push me to do better: I'd think, "I can sing, but I can't hit the high notes she can," and that caused me to spend three months with a vocal coach stretching my voice and adding to my repertoire. Or I'd think, "What a great use of props," or "She answered that question so diplomatically." That type of competition can propel you to improve your own skills.

There's a saying in drag pageants: "We'll be friends again when this is over." What it comes down to is that any kind of event where you're competing with one another, whether that's pageants or *Drag Race*, means that ultimately you're there for yourself. But how far you take that can be the difference between being a lady and being a tramp.

On a small scale, I've seen petty things—like when a girl asked, "Can I borrow your glue to fix my earring?" and it was sitting right out on the table and the queen picked it up, put it in her bag, and said, "I'm sorry. I don't have any."

But I've also seen some *shit* backstage in the pageant world. I've seen pageant girls put superglue in someone's wig, crush up glass and put it in the setting powder so it would give someone micro-cuts on her face, spill wine or Coke on someone's white gown, step on a train so the gown rips, scratch someone's CD back when we had to use CDs for our talent acts, steal props . . . and my all-time favorite: One queen pissed off her backup dancer so bad that the dancer dipped the queen's blending brush in black powder so that when she went to blend out her face she looked like a chimney sweep and had to wash it off and start over as the pageant was already starting.

Half of these were at newcomer pageants where the stakes were low: You'd win one hundred dollars and a used crown and the title didn't amount to a hill of beans. But when some of these girls want to win, they want to *win*, even when that means sabotage. Southern girls are experts on that. We've seen *Fried Green Tomatoes*.

And sure, there are some girls who just don't like one another, but in general, drag is a pretty small world. You run into the same queens over and over if they're any good, and you automatically have a lot in common, so you might as well be friends when you're not actively trying to Tonya Harding one another.

It's "Her Year"

And much like Tonya Harding, *Drag Race* kneecapped the pageant world. Prior to the show, girls put their all into the pageants because that was everything we had to prove ourselves. But then *Drag Race* became a much bigger draw because it meant a much bigger international audience, a way different league in terms of social media and building a fan base.

When it started up, friends would ask if I was going to audition and I said no . . . I was too enmeshed in the pageant world to change my focus. I was doing well and thought

I might be able to claim some of the biggest titles if I kept working at it. It seemed very close.

I competed for several regional titles, and then won two national ones: Miss National Comedy Queen 2012 and Miss Gay United States 2013. But I still wanted one of the "big big" ones, which would mean bigger paychecks and better treatment from clubs.

I competed in Miss Continental Plus (for queens 225+ pounds) four times, each time making it to the national pageant, and each time placing in the top five. I really believed my time was coming that fifth year.

There's a known quirk in the top pageants that you actually get crowned a year or two after the year you deserve to win. It's like they're keeping a list of whose turn it is, who's "paid their dues." It can be egregious, like in a recent pageant where the winner shouldn't even have made it to the top five because she just hadn't competed well, but she'd deserved the win the previous year so they gave it to her anyway. People online were so upset that she was crowned, and that doesn't go over well with the contestants either, who feel like it's rigged.

Keeping Score

One of the main differences between pageants and *Drag Race* is the audience; *Drag Race*'s main demographic is middle-aged straight white women. It's easy to turn on a television and be entertained for a while by people whom you wouldn't normally encounter. Pageants, though, still mostly appeal to the hard-core crowd—the LGBTQIA+ people who are willing to travel and pay money for tickets and show up and sit in an audience for hours. I'm a fan of both, but it's especially nice getting respect from your own community.

In my fifth year at Miss Continental, 2013, lots of people told me this was my time because I'd done so well the previous year. I got so much love from the audience throughout the week, with people stopping me all the time to say, "You've got this! This is your year."

I got a hotel suite for my dancers, one of whom slept in the bathtub and some on the floor because we ran out of bed space, and we put on a spectacular *Little Shop of Horrors* number for the big talent act. Costumes, choreography . . . it was like a miniplay, and it was probably the best thing I'd done at a pageant.

Going into the Q&A portion, I was thirty points ahead of the next competitor and feeling very confident, because Q&A is my thing. I can talk. I don't give standard "I want world peace" pageanty answers; I speak honestly and off the cuff.

I can't remember exactly what the question was anymore—something about a queen who inspires you, I think—but I remember that I spoke about Ashley Kruiz, a fixture in the pageant world since the 1980s who passed away the night before finals after an illness. She had won Florida Regional Entertainer of the Year just a few months earlier. Ashley had been a friend and a big part of my drag life. She was an old theatre gal like me, and she was the one who had inspired me to do the *Little Shop of Horrors* number. I finished the Q&A knowing I'd spoken well, and happy I got the chance to talk about Ashley.

People in the audience were patting my back on the way out that night, saying, "Congratulations—you won!"

And then . . . I didn't win. I didn't even come in second. I was third.

I loved the girls in first and second, but I didn't understand. How could I have lost so much ground on what was always my best category? Afterward, I got the scorecard back and found out: The judges gave me zeros.

They commented that it was tasteless and tacky to talk about someone who had just died. I was floored. But I understood at that moment that they were never planning to crown me, no matter how well I did, and this gave them an excuse.

Ashley's partner wrote to me afterward: "Thank you for lifting up Ashley and making everybody understand what type of person she was outside of putting on a wig and a dress and walking across the stage." So at least it reached the audience it was intended to.

One of the pageant's judges told me later, "Ginger, you know you won, and we know you won. But because of *RuPaul's Drag Race*, pageantry is on a downhill swing and we don't feel like you have enough of a name to save it. Come back next year."

The unfairness gut-punched me—like so many other things in life, pageantry was moving toward being a popularity contest rather than a measure of skill. Who has the most followers on Instagram? Who already has a following we can tap into? But I also took it as a challenge: If you want me to get a name, then I'm going to do *Drag Race*. I didn't know *how* I was going to do *Drag Race*, but fuck it. I'd figure it out. Because now it was personal.

DISAPPOINTMENTS CAN LEAD TO BETTER STUFF

It's okay to outgrow things. After that fifth Miss Continental pageant, I recognized that I'd gone as far as I could go, at least for then. It's not something I'm regretful about, because it brought me some great opportunities even when I seemingly wasted a lot of money. I made great connections and people who saw me perform in pageants would often hire me in clubs.

There were some great parts of pageantry for me: the celebration of people outside gender norms and the expansion of my definition of beauty. It helped me to be more of a professional: I wanted every sequin right, every beat correct, because I thought of it as potential points gained or lost. Even in disappointments, there's almost always something to learn: something that makes you stronger for next time, if you take the time to analyze and grow.

But I also had to brush myself off and move on rather than continuing to chase the same dream. You can hit a point where you realize, "This isn't my path anymore," and then re-navigate. If I'd won Miss Continental that year, I couldn't have gone on the next season of *Drag Race*, which changed everything for me. And if I'd kept chasing it, it could have harmed me . . . too much disappointment isn't good for anyone's soul. So keep things moving; if you realize you've stagnated somewhere, maybe it's time to find a new dream.

Humble Pie

6 SERVINGS

Pageants can be a great confidence boost if you win, but they can be an even greater life lesson if you don't. Life has a way of balancing everything out. That's why I've never allowed myself to gloat as a winner or wallow in pity as a loser. Sometimes your greatest success comes after you've been served a big ole slice of humble pie!

1 pound ground beef

½ pound sausage

Salt and pepper (to taste)

1 cup peas

1 cup diced carrots

1 cup corn

½ cup diced onions

½ tablespoon minced garlic

2 cups shredded cheddar cheese

1 piecrust (frozen or homemade is fine)

1 cup mashed potatoes (instant or homemade is fine)

1. Preheat the oven to 375°F.

2. In a large pan, brown the ground beef and sausage. Add salt and pepper to taste. As it's cooking, add the peas, carrots, corn, onions, and garlic. Simmer for about 5 minutes, or until the vegetables become tender.

3. Spread ½ cup of cheese on top of the piecrust and spoon all your meat and vegetable mixture on top, leaving as much of the grease in the pan as possible. Spread your mashed potatoes in a thick, even layer across the top of the meat, then crown it all with the remaining cheese. Season with salt and pepper to taste and bake for 25 minutes, or until the cheese is melted and your crust is a golden brown. It will set as it cools, so allow at least 10 to 15 minutes before slicing and serving.

11
Mama Ru Comes A-callin'

I was a RuPaul fan from back to her appearance as Mrs. Cummings in *The Brady Bunch Movie* in 1995—a ridiculous character in a ridiculous movie, and she managed to be a real standout because of the way she fully committed to the role. I went to see it with my mother, who seemed to be trying to tell me something with the way she talked about her. My mother was just enthralled by this queer Black man playing a woman and wanted me to know it, and I felt like she was using Ru as a symbol to let me know she accepted me even if she didn't really understand.

I bought Ru's album and we danced to "Supermodel" in the kitchen. I admired the way she elevated drag; it was a time when drag queens were mostly mocked and exploited on TV, and yet she got taken seriously. She'd get a whole hour on *Ricki Lake* to talk about her life and no one made it into a joke because she's so smart and charismatic. Even in the nineties, she was full of catchphrases, but they were good—her vibe was always positive and she was all about teaching self-love and self-respect.

She got respect because she didn't accept anything less. She had this unshakable confidence, and I had no idea back then that someday I was going to borrow some of that confidence directly from Mama Ru herself.

I didn't hear much about her for a few years, until I started working in nightclubs. Even before I was performing drag, I used to work at Parliament House as a runner, meaning that when they brought in acts I would go to the airport and pick them up in the company van.

One day, I got notice that I was picking up Ru, and I was so excited. When she got in my car, the first thing she said was, "Hey! Is there a Ross around here?"

"Yeah . . . there's a Ross. . . ."

Ru doesn't like to travel—she gets flustered by the anxiety of airports and packing, and somehow this time she'd forgotten to pack her drag. So I got to take her clothes shopping for the show that night.

The crazy thing is that she still looked like a star, even in an off-the-rack dress from a discount store. It showed me that so much of image is about attitude: walking with your head held high, the swagger in your step, the confidence in your eyes. It's something we can all tap into just by correcting tendencies to slouch or smile nervously . . . it can help to pretend you're someone like Ru until you get used to the feeling, and then you can do it on your own steam.

Just a year or so later, she was on *Project Runway*, and then *Drag Race* debuted. It renewed my infatuation with her and cemented her place as a real drag icon.

By the first season of *Drag Race*, I knew some of the girls because I'd been involved with pageants and drag shows. I enjoyed the show, but the drag they were doing wasn't reflective of the drag I did—at least in my mind, it was a narrow view of what drag was, and that was high fashion, glamour, and thin bodies. The only plus-size girl on the show was the very first one to sashay away.

So I didn't follow it closely after that, though I admired that it was successful and that some of my friends were being cast. Hitting the wall with Miss Continental came at the perfect time, though, for my luck to shift.

I had met Jujubee for the first time a few months earlier at a charity event where we were both being honored for raising money for a New Jersey youth group. She was very sweet to me during the meet and greet.

"You're so good at this," she said. "You're such an advocate. Have you ever thought about doing *Drag Race?*"

I told her the same thing I told everyone at that time—"I'm not looking for it, but if it finds me, I won't turn it down."

"Well, they need you and you need them. I think you should do it."

A few months later, I got an email from a casting director at World of Wonder. "We got your information from Jujubee," it started. It turned out that she wasn't the only one who had mentioned me. Several others—Roxxxy, Stacy Layne Matthews, Coco, and others I'd grown up with in the drag world—had also brought my name up.

"They told us that you're a plus-size queen who can really hold your own, and that you're great at pageants. I'm very interested in speaking with you."

In my mind, I thought, "Even if I'm not what they're really looking for, I bet I could still get on the show and piss off the people who didn't think I was good enough."

We got on the phone and he told me he needed me to send in an audition video.

"Okay. When do you need this?"

"Wednesday."

It was Monday night.

I canceled everything I had on deck for the next day and asked my roommate to help me video something. The biggest area to film something was on the deck in front of the pool, so we strung up these weird gauzy curtains as a backdrop and I just went for it—dancing, singing, and doing impersonations.

Neither of us knew what we were doing, and this was before all the apps that make it easy to edit. So he just used his phone and recorded one take of everything. It was a mess. My sleeves got caught on the curtains and things kept falling down; it was like a *Carol Burnett* episode, except that I wasn't trying to be comedic. Once we had all the clips strung together, we struggled trying to figure out how to upload it on YouTube and get it to the casting department. It was bad. Truly, truly bad. But there was no time to do anything better, so I sent it off with low expectations.

Then the casting director called me a week later. "Heyyyy! We need to schedule you for your psych evaluation and your background check and all that."

Maybe my audition tape wasn't as bad as I thought?

"Okay, when do you need me to do that?"

"Well, your appointment is tomorrow at eight a.m."

Once again, it was about eleven at night when he told me this, but I made it happen. Then two weeks later, I was in the owner's office between shows at Sleuths when I got the call saying that I had been cast on season 7.

Sandy was *thrilled* with me. "Now, I'm not gonna say this is *because* of me," she said, "but just know that I'm one of the first people who supported you." I love you, Sandy.

YOU'RE A FERRARI

I could have been so caught up in self-criticism that I would never have sent in that tape. But I've learned now that you have to think of yourself as a Ferrari. Of course you have imperfections—we all do. I like to think of my imperfections as dings in the bumper of a Ferrari. Okay, not everything is flattering on my body. Okay, I'm not the best dancer. Okay, I'm not great at managing money. So what?

If you had a Ferrari that had some little dings in the bumper, would you throw it out? Of course not. It's still a Ferrari! Drive it out in the sun and see how that thing shines.

When I have trouble remembering what a Ferrari I am, I like to pull out old scrapbooks and relive all the high points in my life. I highly encourage you to actually print out pictures, keep physical mementos of your accomplishments and best moments instead of just digitalizing everything. Gidget and I keep swatches of our costumes, and we've put them in shadow boxes along with programs or posters or tickets of shows. There's something special about having tangible objects of your joys and successes that you can reflect on.

It's great to approach self-love from the starting point of knowing that you have great value.

"Do you know why you got cast?" the casting director asked me. "Because RuPaul fell in love with you. We all did, because we were watching your video and it was so bad . . . you were dancing around and you knocked the curtain down behind you, and you hit something with your sleeve and threw something into the pool by accident, but you kept going. You were such a star in the midst of the world literally falling down around you."

"Well, that's me! My world is usually falling down around me, but I keep spinning."

"That really symbolizes drag. You have to make it work no matter what happens onstage."

Just before I left, I was calling bingo at the Parliament House when Jiggly Caliente walked through. I'd never met her before, but I called her out, "Somebody turn off the black light, because Jiggly's new teeth are glowing in the dark!"

"I don't know you, bitch!" she called back. "But that was funny, and I appreciate it." She came back to the dressing room afterward and we found out we were about to be *Drag Race* sisters. That made me happy because I really enjoyed her; we became close friends partly because we're good at ribbing each other. When Jiggly reads somebody, it can come across as so mean, but I get her. It's all in good fun.

Soon I was off on a Virgin Atlantic flight to Los Angeles, a place I'd dreamed about and fantasized about and now it was going to be *real*. The plane had a smoke machine and rock music and blue, purple, and pink lights. I was listening to RuPaul's *Glamazon* album on my iPod as the plane took off with all these crazy effects around me, and it was exciting.

"This is the beginning of the rest of your life," the album repeated, and it felt so symbolic.

Los Angeles wasn't what I expected it to look like: It had palm trees and houses styled just like the ones I knew in Florida, which was comforting. I didn't have much time to look around, though, because as soon as we got to the hotel, three things happened:

1. I got metal detected.

2. My phone was taken away.

3. I got locked into my hotel room.

You're not allowed any contact with the outside world while you're on *Drag Race*, and they're really serious about that. The door to the balcony was padlocked, and we weren't allowed to open our curtains in case someone from TMZ drove by and took pictures and spoiled who was on the show before the *Drag Race* people revealed the cast.

They taped over the peephole in the door and all around the front of the door so they could tell if anyone had left their room. If you needed anything from production, you had to slip a Post-it note under the door and wait for them to make their rounds. I would ask to go out to smoke and then wait three hours sometimes for someone to come by and say, "Okay, we have time to take you for a smoke break now."

I arrived on a Friday and we didn't start taping till Tuesday, so for the first three days I just sat alone in my room and watched the Disney Channel, slept, or paced around the room. We weren't even allowed to access YouTube or other web-based shows in case we tried to contact people online there. On the one hand, it was terribly isolating, and on the other, in those four days I broke my addiction to my cell phone—which was liberating. It was a time of deep thought, where I was able to step back from my life and gain some perspective.

There was a door from my room to an adjoining room, and on the fourth day I successfully passed a note under the door: "Are you a cross-dresser? And if so, do you want to open the door?" On the other side was Sasha Belle, who came over and watched the Disney Channel with me. It sure is a good thing *Drag Race* producers will never read this book. Boy howdy.

My experience on the show was better than I expected it would be; I really thought I'd be one of the first to be sent home, but after the first few challenges I realized, "Hey, they like me! I'm doing well! I should keep doing this!"

The low point was the food: The catering every day was reincarnations of couscous and undercooked chicken, and I lost so much weight during the eight weeks that I had to have several of my costumes altered for the end. One day they ordered Thai takeout and I reminded producers, "I have a severe seafood allergy."

"Don't worry! We checked with the restaurant. There's no seafood in it."

Right. I knew something was wrong as soon as I ate it, and I spent the whole night sick. The next day, I had to do a comedy challenge with Kandy Ho, and Michelle Visage said in a part of the critique that wasn't shown, "It just felt like you didn't have a lot of chemistry with Kandy."

"It has nothing to do with Kandy," I said. "It's just that I was served food with seafood sauce last night and I've been so sick that I can't even focus."

I survived mostly on peanut butter and jelly sandwiches from that point on. (And by the way, if you want a perfect PB&J, here's what you do: Start with two slices of Texas toast, mix a pinch of cayenne pepper and honey into your peanut butter and spread it on one side, then spread Marshmallow Fluff on the other side, layer strawberry jam on top of it, stick 'em together, and cut on an angle. Mwah!)

One of the highest points of the season was meeting John Waters during his sketch and getting a chance to start a working relationship. We've seen each other several times since then and he always gives me a big shout-out and a hug, which is a great feeling. *John Waters knows who I am!*

All the way through the tapings, I was happy with the way things were going. I made some good friends on set, like Mrs. Kasha Davis, whom I still talk to on the regular. If ever you're going through a crisis, she's the person to call, because she'll tell you, "I've been there and here's what you can do about it," or when warranted, "Girl, you're crazy. You need to take a step back and let that simmer and come back to it later." She's a very good, genuine person.

Producers kept building me up, telling me how well I was doing, all the way through the finals. I had originally assumed the psychiatric evaluations we went through were to make sure we were mentally healthy enough to be on the air, but I came to realize that they were taking notes on the buttons they could press with us—the producers had stacks of personal information they could use when they wanted to find an emotional moment, like they did with each of us at the finale. They showed my father on video saying that he was proud of me, knowing that he never had been. And even though the producers did that for TV purposes, it was still nice to hear . . . we do talk sometimes now, and to my dad's credit, he never tries to pretend that he had anything to do with my success. I'm glad that seeing me on the show helped him to get a different view on me.

I opened up about him on the show, and although it was nothing I hadn't said to him before, I think seeing it on television was the first time he really *heard* it. My father is a different man from who he was when I was a kid, and I appreciate that we're able to have a better relationship now. He ended up getting married twice more after my mom (first to his dumbass high school girlfriend and then to my mom's close friend), while my mom never remarried. He started a barbecue sauce company with his new wife, Mary Lou, from her grandmother's recipe, and they manage a camping park. They're friends with my mom. Life's funny.

The Minx's Sick'ning Scalloped Pineapple Paradise

～ 8 SERVINGS ～

This recipe from my mom has been a part of our family celebrations ever since I can remember. Over the years, I have made a few slight adjustments. It's extremely rich, but so worth it. (That's why we have it only a few times a year.) I made this for a few of the *Drag Race* girls who came over for dinner and it was a big hit.

¾ **cup granulated sugar**

1 stick butter, at room temperature

3 large eggs, beaten

½ **cup half-and-half**

20-ounce can pineapple chunks in juice, not drained

6 slices white bread, cubed

1. Butter a casserole or 7 x 7-inch baking dish. Cream the sugar and butter till fluffy. Add the eggs and half-and-half and mix. Then add the pineapple and bread, mixing well after each addition.

2. Bake at 400°F for 30 minutes. Serve warm.

3. For 1½ or double recipe, bake for 30 to 45 minutes in 12 x 9–inch baking dish. When done, the top should be browned and bubbling and slightly set. Do not overbake.

4. You can mix this all ahead and refrigerate overnight. Try to bring it almost to room temperature before baking, or plan on a longer baking time if the dish is cold.

NOTE: Slightly dry (stale) bread works best. If the bread is fresh, spread out in a single layer on a large cookie sheet and leave out overnight to dry out some. Use the cubes and all the crumbs that come from slicing the bread. If you try to cut the fat by substituting low-fat ingredients, it will not taste the same at all.

Expecting the Unexpected

Many months go by between taping and airing, which means we're kept in suspense all that time. I kept in close touch with Katya, who was worried that she was going to be portrayed badly and I was going to be America's sweetheart. She was worried about relapsing into addiction under the anxiety, so I used my airline vouchers and a little cash to send her a ticket to come stay with me for a week.

The show finally started airing, and . . . it went about the opposite of what she expected. Everybody loved Katya, who won Miss Congeniality. As for me? Not so much.

It's considered a cop-out to say you got a "bad edit," so I won't. I said all the things they showed me saying, some of which were rude. But the context was intentionally missing, and that was difficult not to take to heart.

What the audience didn't see was that early in the tapings the younger queens had just spent an hour and a half berating Kennedy and me while we sat there and tried ignoring them.

"You're so old. Your drag is so tired. You're never going to win looking like that. You're never going to be amazing. You can't win this."

So I lashed back out and gave them shit about being inexperienced and not knowing anything about drag. When you allow yourself to get your buttons pushed, it doesn't even matter to outsiders who did the pushing; what matters is there's been an explosion.

I had to learn to be more careful about letting trash talk get to me. You have to ask yourself, "How does it serve me to react? How will it come across if I respond to this in kind?" If I had it to do over, I'd float above it all like a Powerpuff Girl. Specifically Bubbles.

Once the producers decided to show that first out-of-context clip, I assumed they'd make it a back-and-forth. Show Kennedy and me being bitchy one week, show the other queens having their bad moments another week. But instead, the "bad moment" clips kept getting focused just on Kennedy and me. Even things that were not actually bitchy were edited to make them look different. Miss Fame had asked me if I was nervous about the design challenge "because you're an actor and design and fashion isn't your thing." It was a nice conversation—she wasn't coming for me; she was asking about it. And then I turned around and asked her, "Are you nervous that there's an acting challenge and you're not an actress?"

I was just continuing the conversation, but they cut everything around it, so it looks like I just tore into her out of nowhere. Then it cut to a shot of her randomly from some other time of the day, looking offended. So I got to be the villain again.

There were moments of tension through the tapings, but some of it got better. Pearl and I started badly, but I ended up liking her; I got to understand her more as this free-spirited hippie who loved the art of drag but not the performance and celebrity aspect of it.

In the beginning, I was the only smoker on set and the producers would let me go outside for smoke breaks. The other girls wondered, "Why is Ginger getting special treatment?" and when they found out the reason suddenly several of them decided to be smokers, too. First Pearl, then Katya un-quit (she'd quit smoking a few months earlier, but the allure of breaks was too alluring), then Trixie Mattel would come out and hold a cigarette and just pretend to smoke . . . soon it was half the cast outside and half the cast inside, and I think that's where some of the drama came from—we got to know one another better in those two groups: the inside queens and the outside queens.

The Disney Channel studio was right across from us, so we enjoyed the fact that a bunch of half-dressed queens would be sitting on stools with our gowns hiked up and then suddenly there would be a line of fifty kids and their guardians showing up for an audition for *Liv and Maddie* or something. The other girls would run inside, but I thought it was fun to give the kids something to talk about.

Trixie and I caught each other's eye when Ru announced the John Waters episode—we were both really excited about that and thought we'd work well together, so we paired up. The first thing she said was, "I don't want to play the Egg Lady. I think they're going to expect me to play Edith, but there's not much you can do in a playpen."

"Well, perfect," I said. "Because like you, I think they're expecting me to play Divine, and that's a setup for disappointment if I don't knock it out of the park."

Edith's "Egg Lady" was one of John Waters' most iconic characters, and I was excited to give it my all. When Ru came over and saw us rehearsing, he was baffled. "Wait, wait, wait. You switched roles?"

"You told us to pick the roles we wanted to play," I said.

"Yes, but I thought you would play Edith and you would play Divine."

"That's the joy of theatre, getting to play roles no one expects you to play."

He laughed. "Okay, I get it."

I think the reason Trixie and I were so successful on that challenge is that they didn't know what to expect from us and they kept pushing us to go bigger and bigger. We didn't really rehearse it; we just went straight to taping, and we taped for three hours screaming the song out while the crew kept throwing eggs at us from off camera—dozens of raw eggs, plus foam eggs and other fake eggs that had some heft to them so they hurt when they hit. At one point Trixie cracked an egg in my eye, and that was the take they used. The crew was cracking up the whole time we filmed.

Over time under the hot stage lights, the raw eggs started to get funky and we smelled horrendous. I stripped down right afterward and producers threw me a robe so we could get my clothes right into the wash. It was a week before that rotten egg smell stopped sticking to my tights. But it was worth it—this challenge was hilarious to work on, and is one of those "Top 10 *Drag Race* Moments" that people keep bringing up.

GET UGLY

It takes confidence to "get ugly." You have to be willing to take the risk of coming across in an unattractive light, whether that's getting hit by eggs or just getting so into something that your face gets all squashed up with passion or emotion. Because those are some of the greatest moments.

Some people seem to be born confident, while most of us need to work on it. But it's worth working on. There has to come a point in your life when you stop worrying about what the haters are going to think and care more about throwing yourself fully into the things you care about.

Peanut Butter Clouds

⌒ SERVES 1 ⌒

I made so many peanut butter and jelly sandwiches during my *Drag Race* time because I couldn't handle the catering, but you can even take something as simple as PB&J and elevate it to something decadent.

2 quarts vegetable oil

½ cup all-purpose flour

1 tablespoon brown sugar

1 teaspoon baking powder

1 teaspoon salt

1 large egg

⅔ cup milk

1 tablespoon vanilla extract

2 teaspoons peanut butter

Honey (to taste)

Pinch of cayenne pepper (to taste)

2 thin slices white bread

1 tablespoon Marshmallow Fluff

Powdered sugar (to sprinkle)

1. Put the oil on medium heat to get ready for frying.

2. In a large mixing bowl, stir together the flour, brown sugar, baking powder, and salt. Blend in the egg, milk, and vanilla. Set aside.

3. Mix your peanut butter, honey, and cayenne together and spread from the center of the bread toward the outside crust, being careful not to have any overflow. Do the same with the Marshmallow Fluff on the other slice of bread. Remove the crust and cut your sandwich into quarters, pressing the edges with your knife to seal as you work.

4. Dip the sandwich quarters into the batter, let it drip off, then dip it again—get 'em good and gooey!—then drop them into the hot oil. Fry until golden brown and fluffy. Place on a paper towel to absorb excess oil and allow to cool. Sprinkle with powdered sugar and devour!

High to Low

Trixie and I were paired up again for the Prancing Queens episode, and I told her, "I'm not much of a dancer. I can pick up choreography, but I'm not a dancer-dancer and I'm a little nervous about it."

They threw us right in with the professional choreographers, though, who had us doing stunts right away without much preparation. The first time Trixie tried to lift me in rehearsal, she dropped me and we fell on a hay bale and I landed on her foot. I was icing my ass, she was icing her foot, they called in medics because they weren't sure if my ass had broken her foot . . . long story short, we were stuck in the *Untucked* room for hours waiting to see if we were medically cleared to go on, and then all of a sudden it was, "Go, go, go!" and we had to rush to finish our costumes and the choreography in half the usual time. It was hard to follow up our really successful act, and we literally stumbled over ourselves trying.

Michelle has a reputation for giving some harsh feedback, but she's really the motherly one on set, and we all know she cares about us and follows our careers. She's invested the whole time, making little comments—"Girl, look at the way you're standing. Put your foot out the other way." "I love that dress, but does it have to be that color?" You can wonder about the other judges, "Did they love it? Did they hate it?" but you always know with Michelle, because she'll give you a running commentary.

My time on the show felt really good, and I felt supported. I left on a high note, knowing I was a contender for the crown. Producers compared my humor to Bianca Del Rio and I thought that was how I might be perceived by the audience—bitchy but fun.

You sign away all rights to your footage when you sign on with *Drag Race*, specifically granting them permission to use it and edit it in any way they wish, so you can't do anything about it when pieces are cut up and twisted around and set to dramatic music. And I get that it's more exciting TV to drive up conflicts and create "good girl" and "bad girl" dynamics, but we're the ones who have to live with the fan reactions and the hate afterward. And boy, did that put me into a funk.

Before the show even aired, just after they announced the cast, I started getting messages online about it. One of the first was: "You fat whore. I hope you sit in the corner, twiddle your thumbs, and play nice with everybody until you get eliminated."

Listen, I knew I was fat. I've seen mirrors. But I was fairly neutral about it until it became a focal point for all the online hatred pointed at me.

Once the shows aired, the hate mail was relentless. Week after week, I'd get messages online and see posts about me on Reddit and social media about what a jealous, fat bitch I was. I was totally emotionally unprepared for this type of fame—like most of the other girls, I wasn't removed from it like A-list celebrities who have other people running their socials. It was me reading everything, figuring out what to respond to and what to ignore, wading through teenagers tearing me apart and hoping I'd drink some poison or something. I still get death threats.

My mom was out there on Facebook defending me when these nasty comments came through. I was thirty years old by then and my mom was still trying to protect me. Thanks, Mama.

The Finale

Shortly before the end of the season aired, I had a dream about my grandfather where he said he was proud of me.

In one sense, I knew that was true—I loved that man and he loved me. But he had drawn the line at *Drag Race*. He would not watch it. At least, that's what he said. I came to find out that he'd added DVR to their cable package just so he could record it and watch it after my grandmother was asleep.

I didn't know he'd been sick. No one wanted to tell me because it was such a big time in my life and they didn't want to mess that up . . . but I called my mama the day I had that dream and I just knew.

"He's gone, isn't he?"

"How did you know?"

I flew home to Leesburg for the funeral, and found a line all the way out the door of the church and down the street. I didn't recognize hardly anybody, so I said to my mother, "Who the fuck are these people?"

"They're your fans," she said—and it was the first moment I realized *not everybody hates me.*

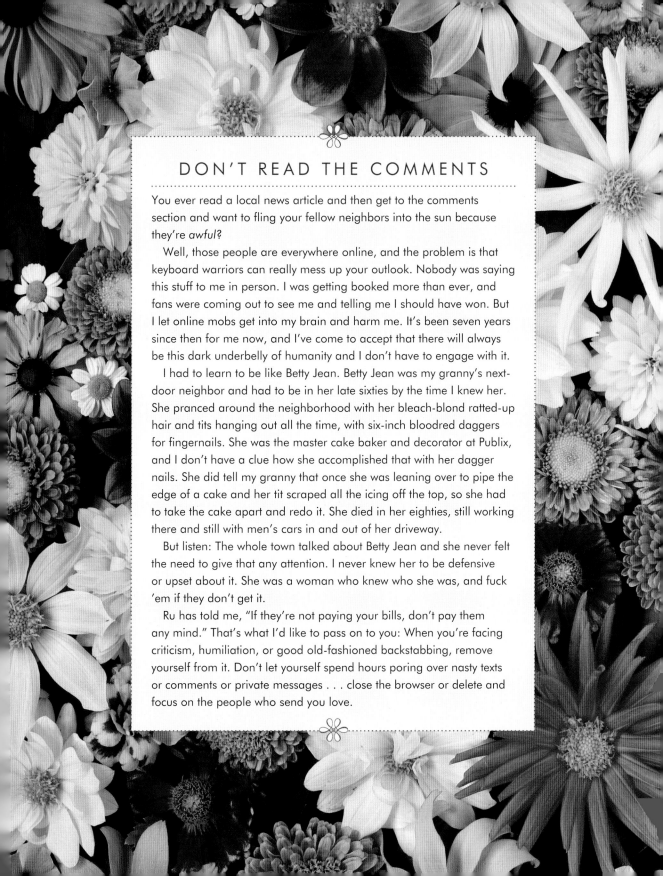

DON'T READ THE COMMENTS

You ever read a local news article and then get to the comments section and want to fling your fellow neighbors into the sun because they're *awful*?

Well, those people are everywhere online, and the problem is that keyboard warriors can really mess up your outlook. Nobody was saying this stuff to me in person. I was getting booked more than ever, and fans were coming out to see me and telling me I should have won. But I let online mobs get into my brain and harm me. It's been seven years since then for me now, and I've come to accept that there will always be this dark underbelly of humanity and I don't have to engage with it.

I had to learn to be like Betty Jean. Betty Jean was my granny's next-door neighbor and had to be in her late sixties by the time I knew her. She pranced around the neighborhood with her bleach-blond ratted-up hair and tits hanging out all the time, with six-inch bloodred daggers for fingernails. She was the master cake baker and decorator at Publix, and I don't have a clue how she accomplished that with her dagger nails. She did tell my granny that once she was leaning over to pipe the edge of a cake and her tit scraped all the icing off the top, so she had to take the cake apart and redo it. She died in her eighties, still working there and still with men's cars in and out of her driveway.

But listen: The whole town talked about Betty Jean and she never felt the need to give that any attention. I never knew her to be defensive or upset about it. She was a woman who knew who she was, and fuck 'em if they don't get it.

Ru has told me, "If they're not paying your bills, don't pay them any mind." That's what I'd like to pass on to you: When you're facing criticism, humiliation, or good old-fashioned backstabbing, remove yourself from it. Don't let yourself spend hours poring over nasty texts or comments or private messages . . . close the browser or delete and focus on the people who send you love.

There was a guest book at the viewing, and one after another, there were beautiful messages of support from people, some who had driven for hours just to show up for me, a stranger. Some said nice things about how they enjoyed watching me on TV, and others were local people who said things like: "Thank you for showing me it's okay to be who I am."

Now, the finale of the show isn't taped way in advance; it's taped two weeks before it airs, which was just a week after my grandfather died. I was a jumble of emotions. When the time came, I flew my mom and sister out to LA to be in the audience; they'd never been outside Lake County before, so it was a big deal. I hoped it would be a time of bonding and healing for us. My sister had done a lot of growing up (she's a special ed teacher now) and I wanted both of them to share in the moment with me.

The team tapes three different endings with the final three so that nobody—not even us—knows whom they actually chose to win until it airs. So in my season, they taped separate endings showing me, Violet, and Pearl all being crowned. Even though I knew it might not be real, I still felt overwhelming joy when RuPaul announced my name as the winner.

There was no bright spot at the end of all that hate for me, because I didn't get the crown even though most girls on my season assumed I was going to. Years later, Violet said in an interview with *Gay Times*, "I truly believe that my season was not for me to win. I believe that Ginger Minj was supposed to win my season, and I'm convinced that the producers of the show wanted her to win, but she was just so unlikable."

It felt devastating to be thought of that way. In the regular drag world, I'm not known as a shade queen at all—I'm direct and honest, but I don't try to make anyone feel bad. The whole thing just hurt. I was dealing with the disappointment of losing the crown and the onslaught of public hate, I had recently ended my relationship, and my grandfather died . . . and then World of Wonder called again, almost immediately.

"Hey, Ginger! We'd like you to come back for *All Stars 2*."

"I don't think so," I said. "This isn't a good time. Maybe another season."

"There may not be another season. When Logo greenlit us, it was for thirteen seasons for the whole franchise, and *All Stars 2* is the thirteenth season. We don't know if it'll be renewed, so it's now or never."

I was so conflicted—I knew I was in no mental state to get back into that werkroom, and I really just wanted to move forward with my life. I had just accepted a $40,000 job touring in Australia and was hoping that would take my mind off my troubles. Travel is a great mood changer, plus: kangaroos. Fuck yeah.

"Our contract says that we can call you back for any shows for three years," he continued. "We're not going to make you do it if you definitely don't want to, but I don't think you should turn this down. We're bringing back the runners-up and the favorite girls from all the seasons so we can go out with a big bang. We'd really love to have you."

I decided I couldn't turn down what might be my last chance to go back to the Runiverse and achieve some lasting fame. Begrudgingly, I said yes and ended my Australian tour. I tried pulling all new looks together and getting myself prepared, even though I was crying nearly every day leading up to getting on that plane.

It was less than two months after they crowned Violet that I was back on set, and this time it didn't feel nearly as fun. I didn't trust how I'd be seen after my portrayal on season 7, and I didn't know most of the contestants this time—Katya was my only friend there whom I could confide in when I was breaking down, which was just about all the time. And then even she seemed to start distancing herself from me.

I felt like a little black rain cloud, on set and off. I was back in that cold hotel room, alone and cut off from everyone, trying not to let my brain go to its darkest places. Mostly failing. But I was trying to find my spirit.

In the confessionals, the producers kept trying to goad me into being more critical of other contestants. They do that—they want you to critique everyone's looks and everyone's challenges—but I just wasn't going along this time. I'd rather be a clown in a gown than a pig in a wig. I didn't want to punch down or go for any low-hanging fruit, and as someone with 54DDDs, believe me, no one's fruit hangs lower than mine.

"What did you think of her outfit?"

"Oh, I really liked it. I thought she looked nice."

"But do you really think she should have worn pink shoes with that purple outfit?"

And then you're supposed to say something like, "Girl! Pink shoes with a purple outfit? Who dressed you, Stevie Wonder?"

But instead I said, "Yeah, it looked fine."

That's terrible TV.

"Come on, give us the sassy Ginger we love so much."

I couldn't. Even the normal things that usually felt funny and lighthearted now felt like some sixteen-year-old was going to hear it and think I was evil and must be destroyed because I just read her favorite queen. I didn't want to be that target anymore, even if I knew that meant I would get less airtime because I couldn't give producers what they were looking for. I was in no mood to be the center of attention. That spotlight can burn.

The challenge that put me in the bottom—the "Baddest Bitches in History" Rusical where I played Catherine the Great—was confusing because the judges' feedback had been excellent. It was like, "You're amazing. You deserve your own show on Broadway. You are a brilliant performer and I couldn't take my eyes off you . . . but you're in the bottom. And not only are you in the bottom; you're in the bottom against your closest friend here. And not only that, but this is the first time where it's going to be just the two of you against each other instead of three." It felt deliberate, like they were trying to teach me a lesson, though I still can't tell you what that lesson was.

It felt bad to be eliminated so early after doing so well the previous season—everything I worked for was coming down to that? But once I was cut, I was ready to go home. I called my mom and told her I was heading to the airport and asked if she could pick me up.

"Honey, I'm at the airport right now. They called me and said I'm supposed to fly out there to meet you to do the makeover."

I realized that they probably intended to call me back on the comedy challenge, but I was spent. I told the producers, "I don't want to be here. I don't think I'm going to be able to give you what you want because I'm in such a bad emotional place right now. I don't think I can compete." So luckily, they were kind enough to let me stay eliminated and go home. But then I kicked myself for years, because it was such a sad way to go out, barely seen at all after having been such a strong force the previous season.

I didn't stay down, though. Once I pushed through the hurt of being eliminated, I picked up where I left off on a bunch of new opportunities. *Drag Race* might have been bad for my ego in some ways, but it was also an undeniably enormous boon to my career.

Matzo Ball Soup

⌒ 2 QUARTS ⌒

Talk to any girl from the show and they'll all tell you the same thing: The real race begins when the show ends. You pack up your sequins and hit the ground running, seeing the world from airplane windows and sleepy eyes. I'm not gonna say it isn't everything I've ever dreamed of, but it's exhausting and can really take a toll if you don't take care of yourself. Anyone who knows me will tell you I've got the attention span of a gnat (Oh, look! Something shiny!), so sometimes I forget to eat when I'm supposed to or take my vitamins. Luckily, my husband is always there to swoop in with his grandmother's matzo ball soup, a delicious cure-all she lovingly dubbed her Jewish penicillin. No matter how run-down or stuffy or awful I feel, a big piping-hot bowl of this soup sets me right and helps me keep pushing forward.

FOR THE SOUP

4 to 5 pound chicken, cut into 8 pieces (2 breast halves, 2 thighs, 2 drumsticks, and 2 wings)

2 large white onions, unpeeled and quartered

6 celery stalks, cut into 1-inch pieces

4 large carrots, peeled and cut into 1-inch pieces

2 tablespoons butter

12 cups water

4 to 5 sprigs fresh dill (plus an extra sprig for garnish if desired)

1 tablespoon black peppercorns

Pepper (to taste)

FOR THE MATZO BALLS

3 large eggs, well beaten

¾ cup matzo meal

¼ cup chicken fat, melted

1 tablespoon chicken stock, cooled

2 tablespoons club soda

1¼ teaspoons kosher salt

HOW TO BREAK DOWN A CHICKEN

Sharpen your knife before cutting your chicken. With the chicken breast side up, run a sharp knife down the center of the breast and slice down, splitting in two. Pull the wing out and remove the first two joint sections by cutting through the socket. Repeat on the other side. With the leg in hand, run your knife between the breasts to cut the skin and separate them. Continue to pull the leg while cutting, follow through to the joint, and cut through. Once the leg is removed, pull the thigh and separate it from the socket. To remove the breasts, run the knife from the top of the chicken to the bottom while making multiple passes down through the wishbone and breastplate and all the way to the wing bone. Cut the breast from the wing bone. Nothing should be thrown away, as all the bones can be put into the stock—they add a *ton* of flavor.

MAKE THE STOCK

1. In a large stockpot, sweat the onions, celery, and carrots in the butter until the onions are translucent. Add the chicken, water, dill, and peppercorns to the pot. Reduce the heat and simmer for 20 minutes. Remove the breast from the stock, let cool, and remove the bones. Add the bones back to the stock.

2. While the stock continues to simmer, shred the breast meat, cover, and chill.

3. Continue to simmer the stock, skimming the surface occasionally (reserve ¼ cup of chicken fat for matzo balls), until reduced by one-third (approximately 2 hours). Once reduced, strain the stock through a fine mesh strainer into a saucepan or airtight container if not being used right away. This stock can be made up to 2 days before using or 4 months when frozen.

MAKE THE MATZO BALLS

Mix the eggs, matzo meal, chicken fat, chicken stock, club soda, and salt in a medium bowl (mixture will resemble wet sand; it will firm up as it rests). Cover and chill for at least 2 hours. This mixture can be made up to 24 hours before using it.

ASSEMBLY

1. Now this is where you can get creative with your soup. Grandma always had carrots and celery in her soup when she served it to CeeJay, but if you don't want all that you can omit it. If you decide to add them, add your vegetables (sliced big enough to fit on your spoon) to a saucepan, add your soup, and bring to a boil. Once it's boiling, reduce to a simmer and add your chilled, shredded chicken breast.

2. Meanwhile, bring a large pot of well-salted water to a boil. Scoop out 2-tablespoonful portions of matzo ball mixture and, using wet hands, gently roll into balls. Add the matzo balls to the water and reduce the heat so the water is at a gentle simmer (too much bouncing around will break them up). Cover the pot and cook the matzo balls until cooked through and starting to sink, 20 to 25 minutes. Using a slotted spoon, transfer the matzo balls to bowls. Ladle the soup over, top with dill, and season with pepper to taste.

3. When finished, this soup will hold in the refrigerator for 3 days or in the freezer for 6 months. When freezing, *do not freeze matzo balls with the soup*! This will cause the balls to disintegrate into the soup. You will need to make new matzo balls if you elect to freeze the soup.

Battle of the Seasons

I went on the Battle of the Seasons tour throughout the US and Canada in 2016, which was a lot of fun. It was a bus tour, so we slept in bunks most of the time and then were able to shower and wash our clothes at the venue or in hotel rooms nearby. Michelle was our host and "tour mom," and every other night she declared it a movie night and wanted us to sit together as a family. We'd take turns picking the movie—except we never let Jiggly pick because she always wanted to watch sequels like *Rio 2* or *Teenage Mutant Ninja Turtles II: The Secret of the Ooze.* Michelle and I picked things like *All about Eve* and *Misery.* Sharon Needles and Alaska Thunderfuck kept picking slasher movies.

It was on this tour that I bonded with Alaska, whom I'd admired for so long. She was different from what I expected; although the essence of her character and voice comes from her, she's far more openhearted and supportive . . . and I've never met anyone who loves drag more.

We'd sit on the bus talking about pageants, and she had amazing knowledge— she could name all the pageant winners, and who got along with whom, and who got dethroned and why . . . the rest of the people on the bus would just stare at us, but I loved having someone with common interests. She's also a vegan, but the good kind: the kind who don't judge you if you're not.

She would offer, though: "If you're open to trying this sort of thing, this is vegan beef. . . ." I discovered through her that I love a lot of vegan food, particularly the vegan chicken skewers she often ordered.

Afterward, I knew to pick up the phone whenever she called; she wasn't someone who called just to shoot the shit or ask for a favor. She always had something important to say.

The tour was the first time I got high on edibles, and that was a complete accident. One of the girls bought some weed-infused chocolate-covered blueberries and offered us some. Now, I've never done drugs—I don't care if other people do—so my first thought upon seeing a bag of fruit is not, "I wonder if this is drugs."

I was sitting there at the breakfast table when she put the bag out and I grabbed a whole handful of them and popped them in my mouth.

"Wait, wait, wait!" she said, but it was too late.

"What?" I asked.

"Uh . . . let's just give it an hour and see how this goes."

An hour later, I was having a full-on conversation with a pack of ramen noodles. It felt like I was floating over the bus.

Michelle was unhappy. "You have to be more careful," she said, and I promised to ask if the fruit was going to get me high in the future. Sharon, Courtney Act, and Phi Phi O'Hara thought it was the funniest thing ever.

"Excuse me, I think I'm dying," I said. "I can't feel my feet."

"No, that's the point. You get high so you don't feel anything," someone said.

I finally passed out in my bunk for five or six hours and woke up just in time to perform that night. I was still under the effects. I remember walking down the stairs to get to the stage and worrying that I still couldn't feel my feet and thought I might fall on my face. It's tough for me to perform when I don't feel in control, so that was a rough night, but funny in retrospect. As long as everyone was laughing, I felt like I must have been okay.

(I did learn my lesson, by the way—when one of the girls' husbands passed around a tin of chocolate-covered espresso beans at a rehearsal a couple years later, I took several but then stopped and asked, "What will these do to me?" "Girl, they're gonna give you a *good night* if you take that many of them." "Okay, then I'm just gonna take one." One was perfect.)

About two weeks into the tour, we had a travel day off. That night in Wisconsin, Katya told me about cheese curds. "Girl, I'm gonna take you out for cheese curds. It's gonna change your life."

"Isn't it just little broken-up cheese sticks?"

"No! We're gonna find a place right now."

And so we went out with Phi Phi to a restaurant where they served cheese curds (always take up the opportunity to try new foods!), and we stayed out way too late. We had hotel rooms that night, so I unplugged the coffee maker and the alarm clock and everything else that might give off light, I pulled the curtains, and I was drifting off to sleep when the room suddenly lit up—*who was texting me now?*

It was a friend of mine whom I'd worked with for years, sending out a mass text that said: "There's a shooting here at Pulse. I don't know if I'm going to survive. This is all really crazy. I just wanted to let you know I love you."

"This is not funny," I thought, believing it was some kind of drunken joke. Then all of a sudden my phone started blowing up with other people texting me: "Oh my God. Are you at Pulse right now?" "Are you okay?" "What's going on?"

I got on Facebook and saw it literally playing out live, and I felt so helpless. It was like somebody had stepped on my chest and I couldn't breathe. I tried to get ahold of my friends who I knew were there, asking: "Did you get out? Is the building still there?" It wasn't until the next day that I finally heard back from a friend who said that they had gone into the dressing room, kicked the air-conditioning unit out of the window, and then shimmied out and down the alleyway.

It was so difficult to wrap my mind around it—this was happening in my hometown and I was in Wisconsin. People I knew were fleeing from a gunman, people I'd danced with had died, and I was supposed to put on a show the next night with a smile on my face like things were normal.

The FBI met us at a venue in Minnesota. They sat us down and said, "You're all moving targets."

What?

"You're a group of the most famous drag queens in the world and we don't know if there are going to be copycat shootings. So let's go over contingency plans for active shootings."

For the rest of the tour, I was always looking over my shoulder, always trying to figure out where I could stand to be the least vulnerable. It dominated my headspace. We all decided that we had to keep going, but it was hard to be at such a high point—such a fun time in my life, where I finally felt we were accepted and celebrated by crowds of people—and realize that we still had so far to go. The people who bullied us in school were still out there, and some of them were filled with hate and ammunition. Aiming at us just because our existence challenged what they had been taught.

It was good to have the girls around me. There wasn't much space to process, but it was moving to watch the world grieving with us. Nothing was the same after that—we still do active shooter drills at new venues, and we're all still aware that another Pulse could happen anywhere—but we have to believe that there's more love than hate for us out there.

On My Own

Once the tour ended, I was on my own to start booking gigs again, and the landscape looked totally different this time. I was getting offers from all over the world, for way more money than I ever could have commanded if I'd stayed on my original path and won Miss Continental Plus. I couldn't even keep track of it all anymore. I got to be choosy about taking new gigs, and I hired a publicist.

People I barely remembered reached out. "Hey, remember when I lent you fifty cents so you could get a soda when you were six?" Uh, nope. Sorry. Mostly, they wanted things from me—someone's autograph, a free CD, something.

Fans recognized me in public. I loved that part. It's only ever been awkward a few times, like when someone decides to sit down at my table uninvited when I'm out eating tacos with my mom. But mostly, it's been really nice. So if you see me, please feel free to come say hi. Bring tacos.

For the first time in my life, I was making enough money to be financially comfortable, and I was able to use that to help my family. After I saved up enough, my mother, sister, and nephews moved in with me in a big house in Orlando, and I felt good to be able to help provide for them.

So I left *Drag Race* feeling very happy for the opportunities it provided, happy for new friendships, and sad for the destructive parts. It taught me how fragile confidence can be; one day you think you're Chaka Khan and the next you're sure you're a warthog—and not the cute one in *The Lion King*. I had to take my training from Ru and keep my ego separate from anyone else's reactions to me. We all have highs and lows, but you have to be okay with you through it all, even when you screw up, even when other people are mad at you, even when everything seems to be upside down.

Little did I know that my story with the show wasn't over.

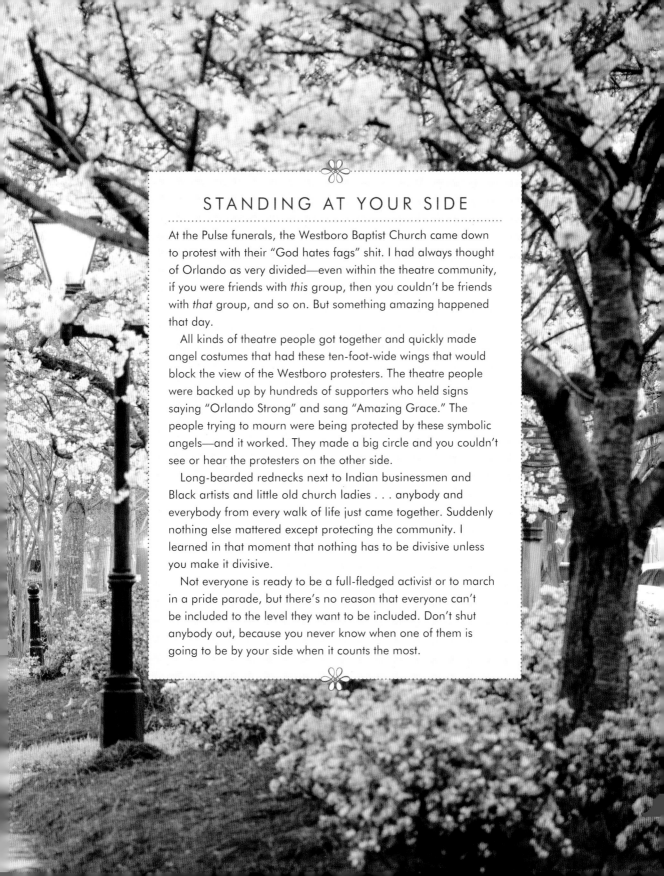

STANDING AT YOUR SIDE

At the Pulse funerals, the Westboro Baptist Church came down to protest with their "God hates fags" shit. I had always thought of Orlando as very divided—even within the theatre community, if you were friends with *this* group, then you couldn't be friends with *that* group, and so on. But something amazing happened that day.

All kinds of theatre people got together and quickly made angel costumes that had these ten-foot-wide wings that would block the view of the Westboro protesters. The theatre people were backed up by hundreds of supporters who held signs saying "Orlando Strong" and sang "Amazing Grace." The people trying to mourn were being protected by these symbolic angels—and it worked. They made a big circle and you couldn't see or hear the protesters on the other side.

Long-bearded rednecks next to Indian businessmen and Black artists and little old church ladies . . . anybody and everybody from every walk of life just came together. Suddenly nothing else mattered except protecting the community. I learned in that moment that nothing has to be divisive unless you make it divisive.

Not everyone is ready to be a full-fledged activist or to march in a pride parade, but there's no reason that everyone can't be included to the level they want to be included. Don't shut anybody out, because you never know when one of them is going to be by your side when it counts the most.

12

Finding Prince Charming

Before jumping into a relationship, every lady must be sure of three things: She *wants* but does not *need* a partner, she has a life and a bank account aside from the other person, and she has a solid handle on controlling the urge to smother the person with a pillow for breathing weird in their sleep.

I was suddenly single for the first time in my adult life and suddenly famous at the same time, which is a confusing combination—when you're not famous and someone's flirting with you, you can assume it's because they're just into you. When you're on TV, lots of people want to be with you just because they want to say they've been with a famous person. You think only rock stars have groupies? The *Drag Race* girls have all experienced it—so many people who wouldn't have otherwise given us a second glance are suddenly locking eyes with us and laughing too hard at our jokes and acting like everything we say is *fascinating* and *sexy.*

We call them clownfuckers because they like us all painted up like clowns. For the most part, they're just interested in being with us in drag.

I didn't like that. I wanted someone to love me for me, and it was getting harder to figure out if anyone was genuinely interested or just wanted some reflected glory.

It came to a head one day when I opened for Wilson Phillips at the big Capital Pride Parade in DC in 2015. I was supposed to do a fifteen-minute set where I'd sing a couple songs to a track, including debuting my first single ever, "Ooh Lala Lala," but it started pouring and their band couldn't go on—so I just stayed out there for forty-five minutes getting soaked in drag, playing with the audience and winging it until it was safe for the band to start.

I pulled a Diana Ross: "It's just a little rain! Where y'all going? Why don't you love me?" and they'd come back and huddle and hang in there.

Carnie Wilson, whom I'd never met before that day, ran over to me afterward screaming, "Oh my God! Oh my God! I love you!" and I shouted back, "Oh my God! Oh my God! I'm tired of being mistaken for you!" She cracked up and it started a terrific friendship that's been very important in my life ever since.

Well, I met a boy at that parade and he came back to my room. And pardon the TMI, but while we were riding the bony express he suddenly turned and said, "I can't believe I'm having sex with Ginger Minj!"

I stopped. I felt ill. "You have to leave right now," I said, and kicked him out. I decided not to have sex again until I felt a real connection with someone.

I still looked around online because I liked the attention and flirting, but I had very low hopes of having another relationship. But then life decided to put me in the right place at the right time. I'm a theme park junkie, mostly because it's a great place to people-watch. I started chatting with someone online who turned out to be a manager at Universal Studios, and I went to meet up with him at the entrance for his lunch break.

"Don't I know you?" he asked.

"Yes, I'm sure you do, like every other homosexual here," I muttered.

"What?"

"From *Drag Race?*"

He stared at me for a second. "You race cars?"

"No, *RuPaul's Drag Race*. The TV show."

"I'm sorry. I don't know what that is. It's a car show?"

"No, it's not cars . . . so if you don't know me from there, how do you know me?"

"Well, you're the one I've been praying for my whole life."

I don't care what you think, that was cute. Even if I thought he was bullshitting me. But I can't help it if I'm a sexual goddess.

His name was Chris, but he went by "CeeJay." We met up for sandwiches. Later that night, he texted me: "Hey, we're starting Halloween Horror Nights tonight and I have to do the switchover, so I'm going to get out of work at two a.m. I don't know if that's too late for you, but I would love to continue our conversation."

I had to get up to go to the airport at 6:00 a.m. for a show.

"Whatever. I'll just stay up," I decided. I picked him up after work and we went across the street to IHOP, talking and talking and talking until I had to leave for my flight. After that, we talked every day.

"Do you really not know who I am?" I finally asked.

"Should I?" he asked.

"Look up Ginger Minj."

He googled my name and said, "So . . . you're legit famous?"

"Well, kind of. Like fame-ish."

"I've never been with anyone famous or anything . . . it kind of freaks me out. But I really like you and I'd like to keep talking."

Every time I came back to town, we'd go to theme parks together—we were theme park buddies. No kissing or touching or anything, just platonic hanging out and getting to know each other and riding roller coasters. Sometimes with other friends, sometimes just us. We knew we were attracted to each other, but I didn't feel like it was fair to start a relationship with someone when I was so into my work at the time. I was gone for months at a time touring and then home for just a few weeks.

I felt like I'd known him my whole life—I was so comfortable around him. He never made me feel judged. I almost didn't know what to do with that. When everything you've known about how relationships work tells you that things will inevitably go horribly wrong, you can spend a lot of time trying to figure out, "What's the catch here?"

So for several months, it was hands-off. But I knew I was falling in love with him. I wanted to cook for him, which is a pretty good sign. One of my favorite things to do in a relationship is to find out about dishes someone remembers they loved growing up—so I ask in innocent ways. ("What did you like to eat on holidays? What were some of the special meals in your house?") And then I figure out how to make those meals. Even when I don't get it exactly right, it's still a great surprise.

CeeJay and I were at Epcot one day, drinking around the world, and we were in the Germany Pavilion when it started to rain. All the tourists around us were running for cover, and we were just meandering around by the lake when he turned and kissed me. Out of nowhere.

"I'm sorry. Did you not want me to do that?" he asked.

"No, I did. I just didn't expect it."

"Well, then you're not going to expect this, but I love you."

"Oh! Well . . . I love you, too."

It wasn't a big, romantic moment. It was almost matter-of-fact. But as I said it, it felt right. Like maybe I'd finally found the real thing this time.

We started dating after that, taking things very slowly. I was rarely at home for long; traveling and touring took up most of my time. But when I was away, I found myself always thinking of him and just wanting to talk to him, and he felt the same way.

When his lease was up, we decided to get a place together. Ever practical, I said, "Well, it has to have two bedrooms, so if it doesn't work out, at least we both have a place to live."

But it was just so easy to be with him. The first time he went on tour with me, he was flabbergasted by the reactions—all these people screaming for me and crying and hugging me and telling me, "I love you so much!" He hadn't even watched *Drag Race* until about a year into our relationship, so he had no understanding of what an impact it had and what the fan base was like. I'd kept that part of my life pretty separate because I enjoyed how he was an escape from that—I never had to question if he was with me for the right reasons, because he wasn't even remotely interested in fame.

I think that's one of the main reasons I've never gotten caught up in the fame of it—CeeJay wouldn't allow me to. He's like, "That's nice. Live your fantasy over here. Take all your pictures and be a superstar. But don't forget, we've got to go home soon because we have three loads of laundry to do. We've got to clean the house before your mother comes over."

It was exactly what I needed to keep me grounded.

We love to cook together. I'm a better cook, but he's a better chef; he graduated from the Culinary Institute of America and is an actual certified chef. He's really good at the technical side of cooking—he wants recipes to follow, and technique, and trips to the store to make sure every ingredient is perfect. On the other hand, I'm the type of cook who opens up the refrigerator and the pantry and says, "I've got this, this, this, and this. All the flavors kind of go together. Let's make something."

That used to drive him crazy. "That's not how you cook!" he'd say.

"That's how *I* cook."

And then he would eat it and say, "Oh, this is so good. How did you know that would go together?"

Because I cook from the heart and I know what works.

But you should try something of CeeJay's, too.

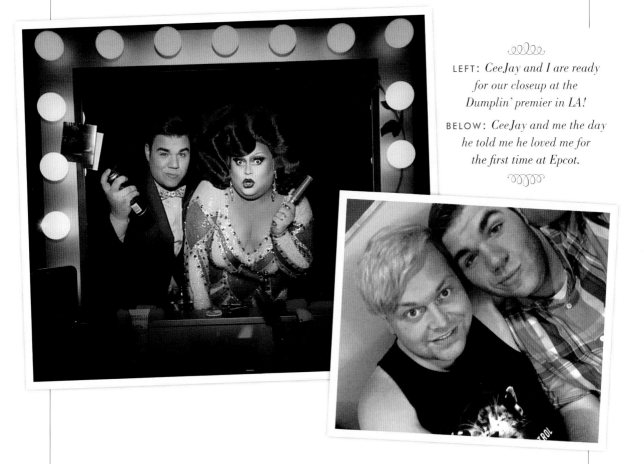

LEFT: *CeeJay and I are ready for our closeup at the Dumplin' premier in LA!*

BELOW: *CeeJay and me the day he told me he loved me for the first time at Epcot.*

CeeJay's Orecchiette Pompadour

∽ 4 SERVINGS ∾

The first trip CeeJay got to take off work to go with me was to my Christmas show at the Laurie Beechman Theatre in New York. We ate at the restaurant, which has a seasonal menu of just a few dishes at a time, and we both fell in love with this pasta dish. He ended up eating it every single day we were there. Then when we returned over the summer, he was pissed it wasn't on the menu anymore—so he decided he was going to figure out how to re-create it. He did! And it's always such a happy memory of our first big trip together.

FOR THE PARMESAN BROTH

2 tablespoons olive oil

1 onion, chopped

10 garlic cloves, whole and peeled

2 teaspoons chopped thyme

2 bay leaves

Several sprigs of parsley

1 teaspoon black peppercorns

1 cup dry white wine

1 pound Parmesan rind

8 cups water

FOR THE BROCCOLI RABE AND SAUSAGE

2 cups water

1 tablespoon salt

1 pound broccoli rabe

¼ cup extra virgin olive oil

½ cup hot Italian sausage, removed from casing and crumbled

2 garlic cloves, sliced

¼ teaspoon red pepper flakes

1 tablespoon salt

1 pound orecchiette pasta

MAKE THE PARMESAN BROTH

Heat the oil in a large saucepan over medium-high heat. Cook the onion, garlic, thyme, bay leaves, parsley, and peppercorns, stirring often, until the garlic is deep brown, about 5 minutes. Add the wine, bring to a simmer, and cook, scraping up any brown bits, until the liquid is reduced by half, about 4 minutes. Add the Parmesan rind and 8 cups water; bring to a boil. Reduce the heat and simmer, stirring occasionally to prevent the cheese from sticking to the bottom of the pot, until the broth is flavorful and reduced by half, about 2 hours. Strain through a fine-mesh sieve into a large bowl.

MAKE THE BROCCOLI RABE AND SAUSAGE

Put the water and salt into a large pot. Bring to a boil and cook the broccoli rabe until nearly tender, 4 minutes. Drain and cool under cold water. Squeeze and pat dry. In a large skillet, heat 1 tablespoon of the oil. Add the sausage and cook over moderately high heat, breaking it up into small pieces, until browned. Add the remaining 3 tablespoons oil, the garlic, and the red pepper flakes to the skillet and cook for 1 minute. Add the broccoli rabe and cook, stirring, until tender, 3 minutes. Season with salt.

FINISH THE DISH

Cook the pasta according to the instructions on the box. Put ½ cup of pasta in a bowl, add ¼ cup of the broccoli rabe and sausage mixture, then finish with a ladle of broth on top. Garnish with parsley and serve hot.

Love and Marriage

Michelle Visage and I were guest judges for a pageant in Chicago when she met CeeJay for the first time. She'd seen me through the end of my last relationship and knew how toxic it was, so she was thrilled to see me move past that. She told him, "I've never seen Ginger so at peace, so happy. She's good to be around. Look at that smile!"

Then she told me, "If you don't marry him, you're a fucking fool."

"We've only been together a few months!" I told her.

"So? I knew my husband a week before we got engaged, and we've been together twenty years now. You're going to Vegas tomorrow, right? You should just do it."

"I just don't think I can get married."

"When you know it's right, it's right. What's the worst that could happen? It doesn't work out?"

I owe Michelle a lot for that conversation because it opened my heart up to the idea of living in the moment and not overthinking things. I was so afraid of finding myself in another bad relationship that I had been holding back. I didn't know how to accept real love; I was waiting for the bad part to kick in. It never did.

Like any relationship, ours had ups and downs, and I didn't always know how to handle things maturely because I was so accustomed to fighting. I'd just stomp off because I was expecting a minor argument to turn into a big battle. But we got through our stuff together, and I learned what a healthy relationship was supposed to feel like.

He proposed to me during the fireworks show in Disneyland, the first time we'd ever been there. We were regulars at Disney World, but Disneyland was new for both of us.

"I didn't want to do it at Disney World in case you said no," he said afterward. "I didn't want to ruin Disney World for one of us. We've never been here before, so there were no emotional ties."

In January 2017, we were in Aspen reporting on the Aspen Gay Ski Week for Logo during Trump's inauguration when producers called us with a crazy request.

"We want to do something to offset the inauguration. How about we throw you guys a wedding tomorrow?" It was late at night and we were in the hotel room.

CeeJay and I were taken aback. "I don't think we should do this," I said. "I don't even have anything to wear."

"We'll get you something to wear!"

"We're in Aspen! There's nothing here but fur coats."

We turned it down because we didn't want our wedding to be a political statement, but producers kept bringing it up over the next few months. They really wanted to be a part of it. *How about you do it here? How about there?* We kept thinking about it and saying, "Nah."

I'd signed on to come back to DragCon that year; I'd gone the previous year and had fun making over Wil Wheaton—it was his idea. He'd gotten in touch with producers

SIX TIPS FOR GOOD RELATIONSHIPS

1. Communicate openly. It can be tempting not to discuss hard things because you're worried it'll start a fight. But even when the conversations are uncomfortable, you should push to have them. A lot of good can come out of talking when people are more invested in listening than just waiting to make their next point.

2. Keep your cool. Contrary to popular southern belief, yelling doesn't help anything. It just puts the other person on the defensive, ready to yell back. No one's really listening then.

3. Stay on each other's team. I don't believe relationships have to be 50/50 all the time—sometimes I'm putting in 70 percent and sometimes he is—but it has to be balanced out enough that you feel like you're always on each other's team.

4. Talk kindly about each other. Don't give in to the temptation to bitch about your partner to other people. Stay each other's fan and surround yourself with people who support your relationship, not who stress it out.

5. Look out for each other. Pay attention to when your partner is struggling or doing too much and find ways to lift the burden.

6. Give each other room. It's not healthy for one person to be your entire world. Give each other the space to have other close friends and family relationships. CeeJay and I still room with other people on the road sometimes; it helps to know you trust each other and don't need to be stapled together to prove your couplehood like one of those "KimAndJose Smith" people on Facebook.

and said he was a fan and was hoping someone would do a drag makeover on him. (When World of Wonder put it online, they initially miscaptioned it "Hinger Minj Makes Over Wil Wheaton," so if you ever see someone call me Hinger, now you know why.) At the April 2017 convention in Los Angeles I made over Jerry O'Connell, who was delightful. And then producers asked us, "How about getting married at DragCon in New York? We'll make it a big event!"

"But we don't want it to be that. It's not a spectacle to sell tickets. It's for us."

Then we decided on a way to make it feel right for us: if they *didn't* advertise it and if it *wasn't* an "event." Instead, we'd do it as a surprise.

We told our friends and family, so they could come in if they wanted to. But everyone else thought they were just there for a sold-out panel where I was making over Lactatia. Instead, they were about to witness Michelle Visage (an ordained minister) presiding over our wedding ceremony. I dressed as Snow White and CeeJay was Prince Charming, and we were both nervous as hell beforehand, watching all the cameras pop up to catch our vows and first married kiss.

CeeJay wasn't used to that kind of attention at all, but he was so good about it, even knowing it was going to be in a bunch of newspapers and on websites the next day. He likes it when fans come over and hug him, but he panics at the thought of being the center of attention.

Married life didn't feel different, to be honest. It just felt good. CeeJay took a leave of absence from Universal to come on tour with me because I was having trouble finding an assistant who could handle all the travel. It turned out he was the perfect complement: I love the creative end of drag, but not so much the business side of things. I'm not great at scheduling, keeping track of payments and contracts, understanding technology, filming things for social media, and all those other pieces that are important to my career . . . but he is. He's just as invested in Ginger as I am, and just as responsible for my success.

The leave of absence became permanent, and he's now traveled with me for four years. The fans recognize him, too, and often ask him for pictures or talk to him about interviews we've done together. He really enjoys that, and I'm so glad there's been support for us as a couple. He's even part of a private chat group just for the husbands and significant others of *Drag Race* girls . . . which I'm not allowed to see!

One of the great things about CeeJay is that he helped me fix the broken parts of my self-esteem. I was so used to my ex telling me that I was lucky he was willing to date me even though I was so unattractive and gross that I believed it . . . I didn't feel like I was an attractive boy at all, and when I'd look in the mirror all I saw were flaws.

Even though I can look back now and say that was about control and manipulation, when you're living it day in and day out it's hard to analyze it for motives—when you hear criticism over and over, you start thinking it's just a fact. The way I came across on season 7 didn't help either . . . I was having such a hard time thinking a single good thought about myself. I felt ugly and unlovable, and like CeeJay was going to figure it out any day now.

My granny used to say, "You cannot see yourself until you see yourself through someone else's eyes," and I never understood that until CeeJay came along. Because when I was standing there in front of the mirror for ages thinking to myself, "I'm getting crow's feet. Oh, my wrinkles are getting so deep on my forehead. I hate my hairline. I hate the fact that I have no neck. Even when I was skinny, I didn't have a neck," he would come up behind me and hug me and say, "Oh my God, look how gorgeous your mouth is. Look how gorgeous your eyes are. I love what you're doing with your hair."

He had a whole list of things to compliment. And that changed the perception in my head. I stopped looking at my wrinkles and lack of a neck and started looking for what he was seeing. "Wow, my eyes *are* so blue. Kind of weird that they're so naturally blue. I never noticed how thick my hair is and how pretty it really does fall."

He changed the way that I looked at myself in the mirror, and that was a wonderful gift.

Once this metamorphosis started, it kept building. Sure, I still have days when I'm tough on myself and have to combat the self-talk that says, "Ugh, I let myself get so fat again. Why am I such a mess?" That's just human. But I started finding the positives even in the things the outside world had always told me were flaws. Yes, I'm short— more like an average-sized woman, which wasn't so bad for drag. Yes, I'm plus-size . . . and that makes my facial features softer and more comforting. I started taking the criticisms and realizing that they were part of what made me stand out.

The right partner will add to your life, not take over. The right partner will build you up, not tear you down. In the South, we can still get stuck sometimes in the "stand by your man" stuff and look at divorce as a sin, but I think the bigger sin is in wasting your life with someone who's going to harm your mental health. You were not created to be miserable. You deserve love. And if you haven't yet, I hope you find your Prince Charming, or Snow White, or Evil Queen, or seven dwarves (hey, you do you).

In the South, we talk a lot about how you have to respect women, but it's rarely put into practice correctly, so southern women have to do a lot of the respecting themselves. The most important love story will be with yourself. Everyone says it, but you have to mean it. What would you accept if you were precious and a prize? What would Dolly Parton do?

FIXING YOUR MIRROR TALK

You can tell someone a million times, "Stop thinking you're ugly. You're beautiful. You need to believe it." But if you don't point out to them *why* they're beautiful, they're not going to find those reasons. They're just going to see that their lips are too thin and their ears are too big and . . .

So get specific with your compliments, both to others and to yourself. Take the time to tell people the positives you see in them so that can become part of their self-talk when they're feeling low. And practice telling yourself the things you love about yourself. Look for the things that are beautiful, the things you like. Focus on that instead of the things you think need improvement.

If you're having trouble with this, channel your inner boisterous southern lady, who always notices something to praise: "Girl! Your highlights look great! Where did you get that done? And that necklace is just perfect with that dress. You have such style!"

13

All Stars 6 and the Country Connection

Drag Race *obviously didn't end* after the thirteenth season—it just kept going like it was *The Simpsons* or something. Producers called me to ask me back for *All Stars 4*, which was nice of them because I figured I'd already had my shot—but I just wasn't ready for it. They called again for *All Stars 5*, but I was doing TV shows, traveling, and enjoying my life and not up for the pressure cooker of competition.

My mom had the idea in her head that I was on an endless vacation because I got to travel all around the world for shows.

"I wanna go with you! You get to see all these exotic places."

"This is not a vacation. It's work," I tried telling her.

Then one day, I had to travel to Punta Cana for a week of performances and CeeJay had a wedding to go to, so I brought my mom instead. We got there and they sent a private car to pick us up and bring us to our luxury bungalow at Club Med, where they'd drive us around the property in a golf cart and give us a private bartender.

"See? I *knew* this was what it was like!" she said, all ready to enjoy some peeled grapes hand-fed by cabana boys.

Then the shows started, and I ran that woman ragged—suddenly the trip was about packing up and setting up my music and styling my wigs and hanging my outfits and everything else that goes into drag, and then meet and greets and packing everything back up again. By the end of the trip, she was exhausted.

"I will never question what you do again," she said.

When producers called again for *All Stars 6*, I discussed it with CeeJay. I felt emotionally sturdier, more distanced from all the hate comments online, and I had always regretted that my *Drag Race* time had ended on such a sad note. I told them I'd think about it. I'd done enough growing to be able to approach it fresh and have something new to offer.

What pushed it over the edge was the pandemic. Just a few weeks after that call was when COVID started raging, venues were getting shut down, and drag work completely dried up. I needed a job. So I said yes.

I was going back to the werkroom. And I was going to do it big.

I felt extra pressure to wind up in the top three because the online comments were already starting up as soon as the cast was announced: "Ginger already had her chance and she squandered it! She doesn't need to come back again!"

I enlisted the help of my best Good Judy, Gidget Galore, to design almost all my outfits. My fashion philosophy is that everything should tell a story. Not every story is beautiful. Not every story is perfect. But when you tell a complete story from head to toe, and in your performance on the runway, it has a lot more impact. Some of the fashion choices that I've made across all my seasons of *Drag Race* have caused a stir, but I still stand by them even if people think they're ugly, because they told the story I was trying to tell.

Frog outfit, I'm looking at you. But it got people talking—I even got memed. When Kim Kardashian wore Marilyn's dress, someone put up a picture of me in my frog suit and wrote: "Kim Kardashian, don't get any ideas." That's because I am exactly as much of a national treasure as Marilyn Monroe, you see.

Frogs and toads aren't supposed to be appealing to the eye on first glance. When you first look at them, they're freaky and bumpy. But when you pay attention to their details, they're kind of glamorous and fabulous . . . which is why I've identified as the Glamour Toad. I wanted my *All Stars 6* run to embrace my journey and how I see myself.

Gidget and I had about three weeks to pull it all together, in the middle of COVID lockdowns, and we were quarantined together at her house. Each day we decided to celebrate a different holiday ("It's Easter!" "It's Cinco de Mayo!" "Fourth of July!" "Passover!") so we'd have an excuse to eat extravagantly. Other people gained the Quarantine 15; we went a little above that. We like food. Mind your business.

My first two seasons were on Logo, and this one would be on Paramount+. All the girls were worried about that—it was pay-to-stream now on a new streaming network, so would we get decent viewership? I wasn't sure, but I liked our new team, even if there were some hiccups in getting them up to speed on what drag entails.

When we came in for press week to do our promo photos, they didn't understand what was reasonable.

"Here's a five-hundred-dollar budget for you to put together twelve looks. It has to look like perfection. And there's thirty minutes for you to do your hair and makeup and get dressed," they said.

They were used to shows like *Love & Hip Hop* and *Black Ink Crew*, where they could just put out a rack of clothes for the cast and someone would apply their lipstick and mascara and they're good to go. They didn't get that each drag outfit is thousands of dollars and we need three hours to get ready. (Well, except for the gorgeous Kylie Sonique Love, who put on a bikini she already had and everyone said, "Oooh! Fashion!")

And of course, at the end of all that money and labor, there's a hot chance it's going to flop for you anyway. I spent $5,000 on my promo outfit and dealt with all kinds of hassles getting it overnighted from the designer in New York, only to have people at home take one look and say, "Hate it."

But overall, there was a terrific difference with the move from Logo to VH1 and then Paramount+. The food was better; the accommodations were nicer; our pay went up; even the vans they had to take us back and forth were nicer.

The confessionals were less charged that season. Producers didn't pressure me to be sassy this time—they said, "We know you're a heartfelt person. Just give it to us from the heart."

That was a relief. And they still showed a few out-of-context moments that looked bad, but I felt like it was a more balanced view this time—good moments and bad. Like real people.

The person I got closest to on set that season was probably Eureka, which surprised both of us because we didn't like each other for years. I think it was fan driven; there's this thing about pitting queens against each other, and in this case there was always an unspoken attitude that there can only be one plus-size queen who succeeds in any season. The token fat girl. One Black girl, one Latina girl, one trans girl, and so on. Like we're in mini-competitions with the queens who look like us. People really like boxes.

When Eureka was cast on season 9, people were saying, "Oh, so she's the Ginger Minj of the season," which I'm sure was annoying when she just wanted to make a name for herself.

Shortly before *All Stars 6*, we were both cast in *Women behind Bars* ("the filthiest show in town") at the Montalbán Theatre in Hollywood. The timing was great for me—I had been working on a tour of *Xanadu* with Jinkx Monsoon, whom I love. But it never got off the ground; we had performed for one week in New York and we were literally packing up the bus to start the tour when the production company said they ran out of money and we'd have to postpone indefinitely. So I was thrilled to get a call saying that Thorgy Thor had a conflict and had to drop out of *Women behind Bars* and they wanted me to play Ada.

It's a role almost nobody wants because on paper it's just *weird*, but I'd always enjoyed her and the challenge of how to make these larger-than-life characters fit into the real world. I loved the show because Divine had done it. And I was excited because I was going to get to work with Traci Lords and Mink Stole and all these other people I'd admired for so long.

Eureka came over to me just before we were leaving to rehearse and said, "So you weaseled your way into this one, you fucking bitch?"

"I don't have anything to do with you," I said. "I don't care what you do. You're playing the lead—I'm just here because I want to get paid to do some theatre."

She gave me a big ole "Whatever," but left me alone. Then something miraculous happened after the first rehearsal.

Grandma Eads' Sunday Pot Roast

↬ 10 SERVINGS ↫

For Arbor Day, I served Grandma Eads' Sunday Pot Roast with mashed potatoes. I still remember when she would put a record on the record player and set out this dish and that whole damn dysfunctional family would stop punching one another for a minute to eat it.

5 pounds chuck roast

1 large yellow onion, chunked

1-pound bag baby carrots

1 large butternut squash, chunked

2 cups beef broth

1 cup red wine

¼ cup Worcestershire sauce

1 stick butter, melted

2 tablespoons salt

2 tablespoons pepper

¼ cup dried parsley

2 tablespoons dried dill

2 tablespoons minced garlic

1 sprig fresh rosemary

1. Preheat the oven to 350°F.

2. Place the meat in the center of a large Dutch oven (a disposable foil dish is fine, too!) and place the onion, carrots, and squash evenly around it.

3. Pour the broth, wine, and Worcestershire sauce directly on top of the meat, allowing to spill over the vegetables. Pour the butter over the vegetables.

4. Sprinkle the salt, pepper, parsley, and dill over entire dish. Once evenly distributed, add the garlic to the roast and rub it all in with your hands.

5. Add the sprig of rosemary directly on top of the meat and roast for 3 hours, or until the meat reaches an internal temperature of about 205°F and shreds easily with a fork.

Sissy's Chicken 'n' Dumplin's

⌒ 10 SERVINGS ⌒

6 tablespoons butter:
4 tablespoons chilled,
2 tablespoons at room
temperature and cubed

1 cup diced carrots

1 cup diced celery

1 cup diced yellow onions

2½ cups plus 3 tablespoons
all-purpose flour

4 cups chicken stock

½ cup chopped fresh dill

2 tablespoons minced garlic

3 tablespoons black pepper

3 teaspoons iodized salt

2 cups water

4 chicken breasts

½ teaspoon baking powder

¾ cup buttermilk

1. Heat the 4 tablespoons butter, the carrots, celery, and onions in a large pot over medium-high heat. Once the vegetables begin to sweat and caramelize, add the 3 tablespoons flour. Allow to thicken into a roux, stirring constantly. Once it begins to brown, add the stock, dill, garlic, 2 tablespoons of the pepper, 2 teaspoons of the salt, and the water.

2. Stir thoroughly. When it begins to boil rapidly, add the chicken. Reduce the heat to medium and cook for about 15 minutes. The internal temperature should reach 165°F and it will shred easily with a fork.

3. In a large mixing bowl combine the 2 cups flour, the baking powder, the 1 teaspoon salt, and 1 tablespoon pepper. Mix loosely with your hands, making a well in the middle.

4. Add the 2 tablespoons butter and the buttermilk. Squeeze the butter into the mixture by hand, kneading the dough together as you go. It should be kinda sticky by the end!

5. Sprinkle some flour onto the counter or cutting board, place your dough on the flour, and sprinkle more flour on top. Let sit for 10 minutes.

6. Pull the chicken from the stock, shred it, and add it back to the pot.

7. Back to the dough! Roll your dumplin's about ⅛ inch thick and cut into 1-inch x 4-inch strips. As your stock boils lightly, add your dumplin's in one by one, allowing each piece a few moments to cook. This prevents your dumplin's from clumping and sticking. Cover the pot and cook for 20 minutes. The stock will thicken and become a creamy, delicious spoonful of love!

"Ginger, I've never seen you in your element like I have today," she said. "I respect you so much—the way that you approach acting, how professional you are, all the homework that you've done . . . I'm blown away."

So we started to chip down the wall between the two of us. We didn't get *close*, but we got closer, and I loved the experience of working on that show. The funny thing about doing *All Stars* together was that even though for the first time we actually *were* in competition with each other, it felt like we were actually there to help each other. There didn't have to be just one big girl—who made that rule? By the end of the season, we had had these big, tearful, hugging, crying lovefests, and I think a lot of viewers thought they were fake. They weren't.

I wanted to say to the fans, "You don't understand how we've spent years of really not liking each other, and realizing now how much time we lost when we have so much in common and we could have helped each other a lot."

It wasn't until we were forced to be around each other that we realized we actually liked each other. So we just let it all go, and now we talk all the time. She's doing great. HBO just picked up *We're Here* for a third season, and I think she's in a place where she realizes she's made it and doesn't have to fight like she did.

Overall, the whole season of *All Stars 6* was much less cutthroat and more support-ive of one another, and that was a relief. It felt like a drag queen slumber party, and the audience appreciated it. My mama didn't even have to threaten anyone on Facebook.

Being generous is a great overall philosophy, both in how you relate to people and in how you host gatherings. We can make life so much more pleasant for one another just by paying attention to other people's needs and wishes. I think kindness is a choice you have to allow—if other people choose not to be kind in return, that's on them. But you're the one who gets to sleep well without concern about how you made someone else feel.

The most exciting day of the season for me was working with Tanya Tucker. Ooh, that was such a surprise. It brought me right back to my early childhood days when I sang on the restaurant countertop: Dolly Parton, Wynonna Judd, Loretta Lynn, Garth Brooks, Patsy Cline, Tammy Wynette . . . and Tanya Tucker. I loved the sound of country music and the stories they painted—you'd really have to listen to the lyrics, and there was always a whole beginning, middle, and end of a mini-play or short story in them. That influenced my own songwriting later, when I told stories about my hometown and the characters in my life.

I'd wake up to my granny playing Dolly music at the breakfast table. She was as big a country fan as they come.

"She would have loved this so much," I thought, and it made me miss her even more. She passed away in 2019. Thinking about her made me nostalgic for the music she loved, and it was like a reawakening.

Drag and country music rarely mixed. It was the perfect timing for a country episode because all four of us finalists were southern girls, but also a reminder that our heritage and our sexuality and gender expressions were often at odds with one another. Country boys in their pickup trucks were not the most likely *Drag Race* fans. And yet . . .

Something in me said, "Why not push this boundary?" It felt right. Drag was getting more and more mainstream—Drag Queen Story Hours were popping up at libraries all over the country, there were TV shows and brunches and Tupperware parties, we were expanding the definition of who could do drag and what drag should look like . . . if we kept letting there be this unscalable wall between the country music community and the LGBTQIA+ community, how could we ever expect it to change? Southern people needed to know that drag was for them, too, and the drag community needed to know that we were allowed into the country world.

"I'm gonna make more country music even if that's super weird!" I decided.

It took nearly a year for the season to air, and I watched along at home like everyone else. You almost forget that you're doing the show for an audience when you're taping it—it's more about "What will be fun to do here? What will make Ru laugh?" That's one of the keys to success—to forget you're on the air and just have fun with it and do what feels good to you. I was happy watching the show and bringing up good memories.

Supportive friends called. Alaska was one of the most enthusiastic. Within an hour of each episode airing, I could count on getting a call from her with a full dissertation on how wonderful I looked and what she loved about the episode.

When I didn't win the crown, she FaceTimed me in tears because she had really wanted it for me. It was so sweet. Again, I ended the season as a runner-up, this time to Kylie. I'm a Kylie fan and am very happy that Ru came around on his feelings about

trans contestants (originally, he didn't feel like it was fair for them to compete, but the fans got loud about it and he corrected himself). It was good to be beside her as herstory was made. Sure, it was disappointing not to win, but I really liked all the final four and felt like we were an unstoppable force: each of us representing an important demographic, each of us an underdog in some way, and all strong contestants. We were all going to be happy with the outcome no matter which of us won, and we agreed in advance that we were going out to a really expensive restaurant to celebrate. Which we did. And we made Kylie pick up the tab.

It was also good to have made a strong showing and to feel like I redeemed myself. The fans did tune into Paramount+, in better numbers than expected. Paramount was good about running a promotion at the time so it wouldn't be too expensive, and we were all relieved to find that fans were willing to pay to stream a series that had usually been included in their cable package before.

Each week I watched my social media numbers climb, and the comments were so much more supportive. I never knew what it felt like to be a fan favorite before; I was so used to feeling sad and defensive when I looked around at comments, and now there was much less of that. You didn't have to hate me in order to love one of the others, and vice versa. We tried to get that across to fans when they didn't get it . . . I don't think any of us enjoyed it when a fan would say, "That bitch should have gone home! You were so much better!" or things like that . . . the *All Stars 6* girls are still a tight group and I hope always will be.

When I did my first shows after the season, I was stunned: sold-out rooms full of fans chanting my name, sending me love. I got to the UK and couldn't even start my performance because the crowd kept yelling, "Ginger! Ginger!" I was in heaven.

Even people from my hometown seemed very proud of me, even if they maybe didn't understand or didn't support me when I was little. Leesburg was still that conservative little southern town, but they liked that one of their own was on television and getting written about in newspapers. Coming home felt so good.

My bump in popularity made me think I could go ahead and take that risk of entering the country market, which I did with the album *Double Wide Diva*. I included a cover of "Friends in Low Places" because who doesn't love that song? But the bulk of the album is original songs, collaborating with singer-songwriters Brandon Stansell and Jeffrey James and producer Aaron Aiken. I wanted to share Lake County with the world—forty-five minutes north of Orlando and forty-five years behind its culture. The good and bad . . . as I'd grown older, I realized how much that place had shaped me, and how its characters had stayed indelibly in my memory. So I worked with the writers on songs that reflected my life story. It was the most personal, vulnerable thing I've done, and my most successful album.

The country world embraced it, writing positive reviews and inviting me to perform in new venues. I started getting calls to record with stars like Wynonna and Martina McBride. The first single, "Walk Tall," a song meant to encourage queer kids and adults to be proud of themselves, climbed up Spotify charts. I felt the great pride of helping to break down a boundary. Plus, it was the first album my mom wanted to download.

There was a lot to love about *All Stars 6* for me, because it gave me an opportunity for a real do-over. It was the right time, and we were all so thankful to have a bright spot in the middle of the pandemic. After the show ended, we were back to pretty quiet lives for a while, while we waited for the world to open back up again. But once it did, it never slowed down. What a time to be fabulous!

TELLING YOUR STORY

There's something really freeing about sharing your stories with people. I think we're all supposed to be able to learn from one another, share with one another, and build bridges of understanding by letting one another know what goes on in lives that don't look like ours. Southern women used to do this just by sitting out on one another's porches with lemonade and talking the day away, but in these busy times it can feel harder to find open-ended conversations like that.

Telling a good story should feel like a mini-movie—dialogue, acting, setting the scenery, big twist endings. You can't just tell people what happened. You have to act it out! With accents and facial expressions and choreography. And the stories don't have to be entirely true. (Except for mine, which always are. One hundred percent. Did I mention I met CeeJay at church?)

My grandpa was king of the fishing story—we'd go out and catch nothing but a few little fish and he'd come back and tell my granny about how he caught *the most giant bass you'd ever seen! It almost knocked the boat over! It was a ten-minute fight to reel 'er in*, and then he looked that fish in the eye and threw her back because he had too much respect for her to eat her. Granny knew to just roll her eyes, but it made for a fun tradition. It's the glitter and rhinestones that embellish the stories that make them sparkle.

Minj's Morning Oats

~ 2 SERVINGS ~

When you're in the middle of a competition, it's important to stay on top of silly little things like food and water, which, it turns out, is often easier said than done. I could best describe the werkroom as a casino in Sing Sing. The oxygen is pumping, there are no windows or clocks on the wall, the exits are guarded, and every choice you make is a real gamble. Don't get me wrong, most of us queens thrive in situations like that (who looks good in natural lighting anyway?), but even though food is carted in and out throughout the day, you're so focused on the finish line that you forget to eat it!

I am the furthest thing from a morning person you could meet, but I had to train myself to get up, do some jumping jacks (I apologize to the poor bastard in the room under me . . . it must've sounded like tap-dancing elephants rearranging furniture!), and put something hearty in my stomach. This is when I discovered my love of oatmeal. It's quick, it's easy, it tastes as good as you want it to, and it really sticks with ya all day! I'm always so sad to think of the wasted years I spent turning my perfectly contoured nose up at the stuff. This recipe is a little heavier and a little more "involved" than most oatmeal recipes, but it's meant to get you through the day without the pangs of hunger makin' your stomach gnaw at your back!

1 cup rolled oats

2 tablespoons butter

1 cup milk

1 cup water

¼ teaspoon salt

½ tablespoon granulated sugar

1 tablespoon brown sugar

¼ cup granola or peanut butter

¼ cup fresh fruit of choice

1 tablespoon honey (optional)

1. Bring the oats, butter, milk, water, salt, and granulated sugar to a rolling boil in a medium saucepan. Reduce the heat to low and allow to simmer, uncovered, for about 5 minutes, stirring occasionally.

2. Remove from the heat and stir in your brown sugar, allowing to cool and thicken for at least another 5 minutes.

3. Okay, here's where you can get creative with it! I usually prefer granola for crunch and either blueberries or strawberries with a drizzle of honey on top for an additional layer of texture and sweetness, but that's totally up to you! I've also enjoyed forgoing the honey altogether and swapping out the granola for peanut butter and the berries for bananas. Honestly, this recipe is so versatile you could have oatmeal every single day and rarely repeat yourself.

4. This is also a great recipe to prepare ahead of time. Make the basic oatmeal in bulk, refrigerate, scoop out a serving every morning, then heat, top, and eat.

14

Put a Cherry on Top

····················· ⌘ ·····················

I finally entered a time in my life when everything was good. I had no regrets about *Drag Race*, I was married to someone who was actually very nice to me, I had my mama, sister, and my two nephews under one roof, and my career was getting better all the time. Can I get a "gaymen"?

And so this is the part of the book where I think we should celebrate. You know how southerners celebrate, right? With dessert!

Oh, it's not just how we *celebrate*. It's also how we commiserate, support, apologize, and show our love. Basically any strong emotion can be paired with a dessert. If you're sick, we don't bring you chicken soup . . . we bring you pie, or soufflé, or cookies. Because that's the special thing. You can get a can of Campbell's soup at any drugstore, but you're not going to find my grandpa's Better Than Sex Cake there. It was Granny's recipe, but grandpa refined it and renamed it. She could make it, but he often did the honors. And no, it's not at all weird that my grandpa taught me how to make Better Than Sex Cake.

At my granny's house, the dessert table was always bigger than the dinner table. And halfway through any meal, you could be sure to hear: "Now, save some room for dessert. Don't go spoilin' your appetite."

Southerners all have their own recipes for pecan pie, so you might have three different pecan pies at any holiday table. Plus a couple coconut cakes, banana pudding, and pumpkin pie. 'Course, after a couple years people start to notice, "You know, Cousin Jamie's banana pudding is all gone and nobody touched mine," and then the following year that person is bringing the mac 'n' cheese instead. They figure it out. If you're really a terrible cook, we make you bring the drinks.

Granny's Picture-Perfect Coconut Cake

∽ 8 SERVINGS ∾

My mom once cut out a picture of a coconut cake from a magazine and stuck it on the refrigerator. She's not a baker, so I'm assuming she was intending to take it to the bakery and ask them to make one like it for her, but my granny decided to surprise her instead. She took the picture to Miss Betty Jean along the way and asked her if she had a recipe. Well, of course she did.

My grandma kept practicing and tweaking the recipe until it looked just like the picture, and then she made it for my mama for Christmas that year.

FOR THE CAKE

1 cup buttermilk

6 large egg whites

2 sticks unsalted butter,
at room temperature

2 cups granulated sugar

1 cup sweetened coconut
flakes

1½ teaspoons vanilla extract

1 teaspoon coconut extract

3 cups all-purpose flour

1½ teaspoons baking powder

¼ teaspoon baking soda

½ teaspoon salt

¼ cup water

1 cup cream of coconut

½ cup milk or heavy cream

FOR THE ICING

1 pound (2 blocks) cream
cheese

2 tablespoons unsalted butter,
at room temperature

¼ cup cream of coconut

¼ teaspoon cream of tartar

1½ teaspoons vanilla extract

2 cups powdered sugar

2 cups sweetened coconut
flakes

1. Preheat the oven to 350°F and grease two 9-inch round cake pans.

2. Whisk together the buttermilk with your egg whites in a medium bowl and set aside.

3. In a large mixing bowl, cream together the butter, sugar, coconut flakes, and vanilla and coconut extracts.

4. Add the flour, baking powder, baking soda, and salt to the mixture and blend well. Slowly incorporate your egg white mixture into the rest of your batter, blending until your batter is smooth. Use the water to smooth or thin out your batter as needed.

5. Fill the cake pans about three-quarters full and bake for 25 to 28 minutes, until the top is golden brown and a toothpick inserted in the center comes out clean.

6. Mix together the cream of coconut and milk. Poke holes gently through the cakes with a fork and pour your soaking mixture over them to absorb.

7. Move to a cooling rack and allow to rest while making your icing.

8. In a large mixing bowl, beat together the cream cheese, butter, cream of coconut, cream of tartar, and vanilla. Once blended, incorporate your powdered sugar slowly until everything is well mixed and velvety smooth.

9. Put one-third of the icing on top of your bottom layer of cake and spread into an even layer. Stack the other layer on top and smooth the rest of the icing evenly over the rest of the cake.

10. Take the shredded coconut and pack it into every surface of the cake until it is fully covered. Place in the refrigerator to set for about 1 hour.

The Big Bad Bear Claw

⌒ 4 SERVINGS ⌒

FOR THE DOUGH

2 sticks unsalted butter

1 packet (¼ ounce) active dry yeast

¼ cup warm water

¼ cup granulated sugar

3 large egg yolks

½ teaspoon salt

5 ounces evaporated milk

3⅓ cups all-purpose flour

FOR THE FILLING

1 stick unsalted butter, at room temperature

1⅓ cups powdered sugar

⅔ cup all-purpose flour

8 ounces almond paste

3 large egg whites

¾ cup finely chopped almonds

¼ cup sliced almonds (to sprinkle on top)

1. Melt the 2 sticks butter and then let cool to room temperature. Dissolve the yeast in water, then stir in the ¼ cup sugar, the egg yolks (save the whites for the filling), salt, evaporated milk, and butter. Stir into the 3⅓ cups flour and mix well. Cover and chill for at least 12 hours. Meanwhile, you can make the almond filling, and then when you are ready to make the bear claws let the filling sit out at room temperature for 1 hour to make it easier to spread.

2. Smoothly blend together the 1 stick butter and the powdered sugar. Add the ⅔ cup flour and the almond paste. Stir until crumbly and evenly mixed, then beat in 2 of the egg whites. Stir in the chopped almonds. Cover and chill until firm.

3. To form the bear claws, roll out the dough on a well-floured surface (use about ½ cup flour) to a 27 x 13½-inch rectangle.

4. Cut the rectangle lengthwise into 3 strips (4½ inches wide).

5. Divide the almond paste into three portions and roll each into a 27-inch rope on a floured board. Lay one filling rope in the center of each strip of dough and flatten slightly.

6. Fold long sides of each strip over filling, overlapping slightly.

7. Cut each filled strip into 6 (4½ inch long) segments. Arrange on a greased baking sheet. With a sharp floured knife, make a row of cuts halfway across each segment and about ½ inch apart. Curve each bear claw so it fans out.

8. Lightly beat the remaining 1 egg white and brush over the bear claws, then top with the sliced almonds. Let rise for 20 minutes, then bake at 375°F for 13 to 15 minutes, or until lightly golden brown. Transfer to a wire rack to cool.

Bitchin' Blueberry Bars

∽ 10 SERVINGS ∽

We used to go wild blueberry picking with my grandfather in a little Georgia town not too far from the Okefenokee Swamp. He'd bring as many of the grandkids who wanted to come and give us these giant pickle tubs to collect as many blueberries as we could find. He would sell them for a few dollars a bucket at a farm and give us half the money that we made for the buckets that we collected.

We'd stop at an ice-cream or fudge stand on the way back to Leesburg and blow all the money by the time we made it back, but that was the fun of it. We'd save just one bucket for my grandmother to make her amazing blueberry bars.

FOR THE CRUST

2 sticks cold salted butter

2½ cups all-purpose flour

3 tablespoons Splenda or sugar

2 teaspoons lemon zest

½ teaspoon salt

1 large egg

¼ cup vegetable oil

FOR THE FILLING

3 cups fresh blueberries

1 cup Splenda or sugar

1½ tablespoons cornstarch

1 tablespoon lemon juice

1 teaspoon lemon zest

1. Preheat the oven to 375°F. Grease and line a 9 x 9-inch pan with parchment paper that hangs at least 1 inch over each side.

2. Cube the butter. In a large bowl, beat the flour, Splenda, lemon zest, and salt together. Add the butter and beat until completely incorporated. You should have a fine, sandy texture to your mixture. Add the egg and oil to the mixture.

3. Scoop out one-third of the mixture, press into a bowl, and refrigerate until needed.

4. Press the remaining two-thirds of the mixture into the pan. Make sure it is as compact as possible to give your bars a sturdy crust.

5. Toss the blueberries, Splenda, cornstarch, lemon juice, and zest together until evenly coated.

6. Spread the berries over the crust. Remove the remaining crust mixture from the refrigerator and sprinkle large clumps over the berries.

7. Bake until golden brown (about 1 hour), then allow to cool, in the pan, for about 2 hours. Using the overhang of parchment paper, remove the dessert, cut into bars, and serve.

Aunt Glenda Faye's Cherry Cobbler

⌒ 6 SERVINGS ⌒

1 stick unsalted butter, melted

1 cup all-purpose flour

¾ cup granulated sugar

¼ cup brown sugar

1 teaspoon baking powder

1 cup milk

21-ounce can cherry pie filling

Juice of ½ orange

1 teaspoon chopped fresh mint (to sprinkle on top)

Scoop of vanilla ice cream (optional)

1. Preheat the oven to 350°F.

2. Pour the butter into a 9 x 9-inch baking dish and tilt it until it coats the bottom and sides evenly. Place inside the oven to warm while you mix your dry ingredients.

3. In a large mixing bowl, combine the flour, granulated sugar, brown sugar, and baking powder with a fork. Once blended, slowly stir the milk into your mixture.

4. Remove the baking dish from the oven and dump your mixed ingredients into it. ***Don't stir it!***

5. Spoon the cherry filling evenly onto your batter, once again avoiding any stirring.

6. Squeeze your orange half over everything, then sprinkle the mint on top.

7. Bake for 45 to 55 minutes, or until golden brown. Spoon and serve hot with a scoop of your favorite vanilla ice cream, if using.

Better Than Sex Cake

∽ 8 SERVINGS ∽

It's been said that men think about sex something like every seven seconds. Who's having it, who they're having it with, and when can they have it again? I suppose for some it can be all-consuming, justified by our constant want to primp, preen, and impress. In the South, we call this peacocking. Granny, however, always lived by the adage "the way to a man's heart is through his stomach." She said anyone could play fast and loose, but cookin' took skill.

Every time my granddaddy had a particularly hard day or found himself in a bit of a snit, my granny would make him his favorite cake. She, being ever the genteel lady, always called it her Banana Split Sundae Special, but Grandpa just called it Better Than Sex! She credits that cake for keeping them together for all those years. One bite and I'm sure you'll agree . . . it's better than any love potion on the market!

3 to 4 bananas (depending on size)

2 cups all-purpose flour

3½ teaspoons baking powder

1 teaspoon iodized salt

2 cups granulated sugar

1 stick unsalted butter, at room temperature

3 large eggs

1 teaspoon vanilla extract

1 cup milk

15-ounce can crushed pineapple

5.1-ounce box instant vanilla pudding

8-ounce container Cool Whip

1 cup chopped pecans or walnuts

10-ounce jar long-stemmed maraschino cherries

1. Preheat the oven to 350°F. Grease a 12 x 12-inch pan generously.

2. Slice the bananas into ¼-inch slices. Mix the flour, baking powder, and salt in a medium mixing bowl. Set aside.

3. Cream 1½ cups of the sugar and the butter in a large bowl. Add the eggs, one at a time, and the vanilla. Alternate adding the flour mixture and the milk until combined smoothly. Pour the batter into the pan and shake to get out all the air bubbles.

4. Bake for 40 minutes, or until a knife inserted in the center comes out clean.

5. Pour the can of pineapple and the remaining ½ cup sugar into a small pot. Heat on high until the mixture comes to a full boil. Reduce the heat to low and allow to cook for 5 minutes.

6. Prepare the vanilla pudding in separate bowl, as directed on the package, and set in the fridge to chill. When your cake is done, poke holes throughout with a fork.

7. Pour the pineapple syrup over the hot cake and allow to soak in. Allow to cool! Place the bananas in a solid, single layer across the top of the cake. Spread the vanilla pudding in a single layer across the top of the bananas. Dollop Cool Whip in a thick layer, creating peaks and valleys as you go. Sprinkle the nuts over the top of the Cool Whip. Place the maraschino cherries in the peaks and valleys of the Cool Whip. Chill the entire cake for 30 minutes and serve.

15

Don't Block
Your Blessings

Even long after my* Drag Race *fame began, I still didn't understand my worth. I didn't try to negotiate terms; I continued doing local events for the same kind of pay as before, and I had been willing to accept less money and worse terms than most of the other queens—partly because it's very un-southern to tell someone to pay you more, and partly because I didn't know any better for a while about what other girls got paid and what was possible.

We all had private Facebook pages and group chats, though, where we'd text one another and make voice recordings when we were too lazy to type. We'd compare notes about everything—clubs, promoters, audiences—and eventually someone brought up money. I realized that I nearly won season 7 and yet I was getting paid thousands of dollars less than many of the others. I had almost accepted that I was worth less because I was fat, because that's what I'd been conditioned to believe. All those years when club managers decided I couldn't be a headliner had taken a toll.

A club out of state would call and say, "We want to offer you an exclusive contract for three bookings a year for five thousand dollars," and I'd think, "Well, I'm used to making a hundred dollars for a two-hour show at Hamburger Mary's, so that sounds fair." Then I came to find out that four other queens on my first season were making $15,000 for the exact same contract.

The final straw for me was a local club, though. For their annual White Party, which was a top-shelf event, they invited my fellow *Drag Race* finalists and me to perform. They offered the other girls $10,000, and they offered me $1,500. Because I was a local girl.

That was it. I walked right into the office and said, "I know everyone else is being offered more money. This is making me feel like I'm not respected and valued, and I can't let myself feel that way. You should not be paying me less because I'm local; you should be paying me more because I've been making money for you all along, since before any TV show."

"You're family!" he told me. "Over the course of the week you work here, you're going to make the same money."

"That's not the point. I don't want to make the same amount in a week that the others are making in one night. I'd rather work one night, too."

BLESS YER HEART AND PAY ME, BITCH

Trixie Mattel likes to say, "Know your worth and demand three times as much."

Southern culture teaches us to be pleasant and polite and agreeable, but that can also make us into doormats when it comes to business deals. And there is a growing divide between the 1 percenters and the rest of us that represents the dynamic between those who hire and those who get hired.

First, just be willing to negotiate. Don't agree to the first figure you hear; that's often just a starting point. Say, "Let me think about it and get back to you."

Second, try to exchange information with others in your field. Get to learn what's normal and don't undercut anyone—it doesn't help in the long run if you undercharge. It just drags everyone's pay down.

Go into negotiations with the mindset that you're going to be loud *and* polite. Be prepared with why you deserve more, and be willing to walk if you don't get what you should.

Then overdeliver. When you show up early, bring your A game, and make everyone happy, they'll be more likely to be willing to pay you what you want.

It took some back-and-forth, but I left that room with the same contract the other girls had, and it taught me a lesson: Even when it was uncomfortable, I had to stand up for what I was worth. Once I hooked up with a management company, they started taking over my bookings and I didn't have to do much negotiating myself. But our culture has made talking about money this weird taboo, and we're all better off when we lift the curtain and help one another get a fair share.

I also had to learn how to crunch numbers to see what was paying off for me and what wasn't. I enjoyed going to DragCons and doing panels, but we didn't get our expenses covered for those appearances, so after paying for airfare and hotels and clothes I realized I was often losing money by going to them. The trade-off was getting to see so many fans, which I enjoy, but it wasn't even the best atmosphere for that—by virtue of how big the events are, you don't get personal interactions. You get: "Hi! Thanks for coming!" and a selfie, over and over. So I didn't sign on again last year. We all have to be protective of our time, our most valuable commodity.

My granny used to say, "Don't block your blessings." The older I got, the more I took that to heart. *Don't get in your own way. Don't worry about what other people have that you don't have. Let them live their lives how they see fit, and you just take care of your own.* We hold ourselves back from living our most authentic lives when we care too much about what other people think and try to force our dreams into other people's boxes.

One day I was crying about a part I didn't get—as a performer, you're never going to live a life free of rejection or criticism; that's part of the game for all of us—and CeeJay asked what was wrong. I told him but then said not to worry about my emotions. "If you've never cried about your dreams, then your dreams are too small."

I could have blocked my blessings many times over when people offered me things I didn't think I was ready for. Early in my drag career, I showed up to a nightclub gig thinking I was just there to perform, and then found out just beforehand that my manager had agreed to have me host. I'd never hosted before! That's not a skill you're supposed to come up with on the spot. But my friend Chantel gave me a little pep talk. "Just talk to them like you're talking to me."

"But there's a lot of them."

"Doesn't matter. Pick one of them and pretend you're talking to me."

I could have refused, or said there was a misunderstanding, but I got out there and just started improvising.

"You know, it costs a lot of money to look this cheap," I said, and someone held up a dollar for me. "Oh, a dollar! That's almost four quarters. I could do almost a whole load of laundry with that." It was something I'd heard my granny say, and the people laughed. Hey, maybe I could do this after all!

Nowadays I love hosting; it's something I developed and realized I was good at, but there always has to be that first time when you're taking the risk of falling on your face. Otherwise, you never get to find out what else you might enjoy.

It was such a turnaround from my days as a quiet kid. My father had taught me not to talk and draw attention to myself because I was so embarrassing to him, and now not only am I allowed to talk, but I'm getting paid to talk also.

∼ℓℓ∽

I have worked with girls who are wonderful professionals, who show up prepared and stay late for every meet and greet with fans, and others who roll in when they feel like it, give everyone attitude, and rush out with sunglasses on so they don't have to talk to anyone. It's not always who you'd think either—the biggest stars are often the most gracious ones. If you expect staying power in any performing field, it's the fans who keep you there, and connecting with them is important.

I've now gotten to work with many bona fide stars in and out of the drag world, and one of the things that's been exciting to find out is that every one of them has been wonderful. The set on *Dumplin'* was so supportive and amazing. When I first arrived for rehearsal and was sitting outside the wardrobe trailer, Kathy Najimy ran out to welcome me.

"We're so excited you're here!" she said. "Come on, I have to introduce you to somebody."

She took me by the hand and knocked on the big trailer door. Jennifer Aniston answered.

"Ginger! We're so honored you're doing our movie," she said.

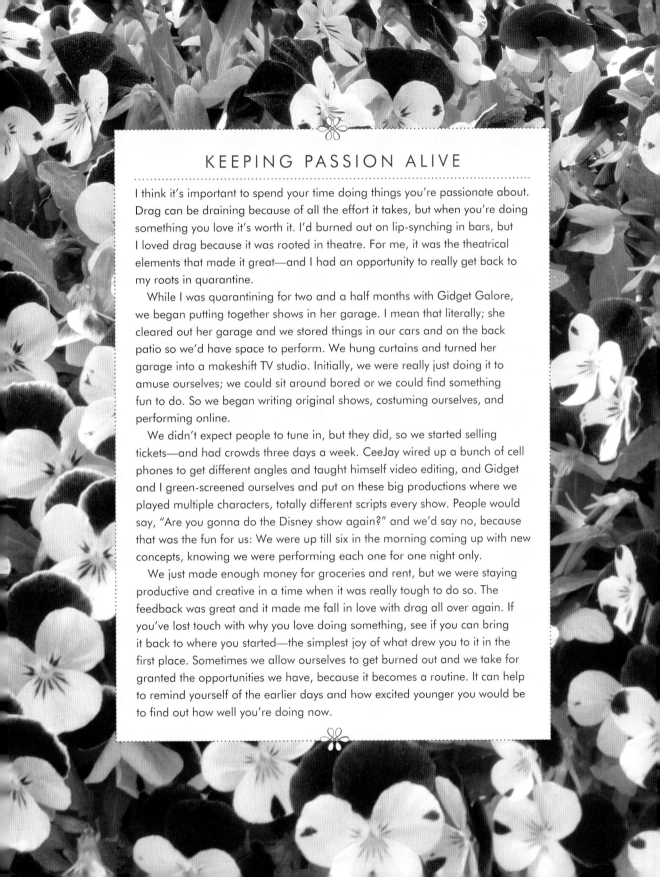

KEEPING PASSION ALIVE

I think it's important to spend your time doing things you're passionate about. Drag can be draining because of all the effort it takes, but when you're doing something you love it's worth it. I'd burned out on lip-synching in bars, but I loved drag because it was rooted in theatre. For me, it was the theatrical elements that made it great—and I had an opportunity to really get back to my roots in quarantine.

While I was quarantining for two and a half months with Gidget Galore, we began putting together shows in her garage. I mean that literally; she cleared out her garage and we stored things in our cars and on the back patio so we'd have space to perform. We hung curtains and turned her garage into a makeshift TV studio. Initially, we were really just doing it to amuse ourselves; we could sit around bored or we could find something fun to do. So we began writing original shows, costuming ourselves, and performing online.

We didn't expect people to tune in, but they did, so we started selling tickets—and had crowds three days a week. CeeJay wired up a bunch of cell phones to get different angles and taught himself video editing, and Gidget and I green-screened ourselves and put on these big productions where we played multiple characters, totally different scripts every show. People would say, "Are you gonna do the Disney show again?" and we'd say no, because that was the fun for us: We were up till six in the morning coming up with new concepts, knowing we were performing each one for one night only.

We just made enough money for groceries and rent, but we were staying productive and creative in a time when it was really tough to do so. The feedback was great and it made me fall in love with drag all over again. If you've lost touch with why you love doing something, see if you can bring it back to where you started—the simplest joy of what drew you to it in the first place. Sometimes we allow ourselves to get burned out and we take for granted the opportunities we have, because it becomes a routine. It can help to remind yourself of the earlier days and how excited younger you would be to find out how well you're doing now.

When I came back to film a week later, Kathy had moved my trailer next to hers, and we'd get ready every morning listening to Beyoncé because that's what she liked to do. Jennifer knocked on the door the first day of filming.

"I read in an interview that you really like coffee, so I had this made for you," she said, handing me a fresh cup of coffee.

After that, she did it every day: Jennifer Aniston brought me coffee. It was surreal.

Dolly was even better than you'd hope. Sweeter, more gracious, and she smells like the color pink. I have never met someone with a better work ethic; she'd roll up at the crack of dawn in full makeup, ready to shoot while the rest of us were still sipping coffee and wandering around in a daze. She would make wisecracks about us being lazy. She gets up around 3:00 a.m. every day, and is always in heels and ready to be seen.

It was actually my second time meeting Dolly in person. The first was when I was seven and my family went to Dollywood. Even though Disney World was closer, it was too expensive. Dollywood had two-days-for-one deals over the summer, so we went there instead. One day, Dolly gave a surprise performance at her brother's show and then stuck around to sign autographs and sell T-shirts. I was fussing on line because it had been a long day, I guess, and she yelled out, "I'm the only diva allowed here, honey. Cut it out!"

When I got up to the front of the line for my autograph, she said, "Anyone who can out-whine me is going to be a star, pumpkin."

I reminded her of that on the *Dumplin'* set. "See? I've been working all this time on getting to be a star because I didn't want to disappoint you."

She pretended she remembered our meeting. Come on, there's no way. Is there?

All the actors were consummate professionals and so welcoming. The whole cast made it a great experience.

The same thing happened years later on *Hocus Pocus 2*, where I got to work with Kathy again! Kornbread Jeté, Kahmora Hall, and I were playing the drag versions of the Sanderson Sisters, and we were together all the time on set in Newport, Rhode Island. Our holding room was in the same place where they filmed *Amistad*, one of the oldest government buildings still in existence. There was still an original portrait of George Washington hanging upstairs.

I'm super into ghost hunting, Ouija boards, and all that supernatural stuff (I may not be light as a feather, but I'm usually stiff as a board), so we spent all our free time wandering around this giant building, looking for ghosts using a ghost-hunting app. One day around three in the morning, the director called over the speakers, "Can we get the queens? Where are the queens?"

Kathy said, "Last time I saw them, they were in the basement ghost hunting."

So they sent a whole crew down to find us, where we were having a conversation with a ghost girl. When we emerged, Bette Midler said, "I don't care what you find—just don't tell me about it."

The atmosphere on set was so much fun again. Kathy had told Bette to watch *Drag Race* before we got there and Sarah Jessica Parker had watched every season, so they knew exactly who we were and they were *invested* in the show and had strong opinions about who should and should not have won.

It was beautiful the way they treated us like they were our fans, and not the other way around. They never treated us like set dressing, but like equals. I think we caught Disney's corporate people by surprise, too, when they saw how we got swarmed with paparazzi when we arrived—they hadn't planned for security for us because I don't think they realized how big the *Drag Race* fan base is. The second day, we had full security detail just like the main witches.

I had the same "tooth stylist" as Bette had in the original movie, and the prosthetic teeth were ridiculous. Our costume designers spared no expense; the costumer showed me that the silk and beaded lace on my dress were hundreds of dollars per yard, adding up to a cost of almost $15,000 to make the dress. It was probably the most extravagant thing I've ever had on my body. At the end, the designers cut swatches of the fabric from each of our costumes and gave us shadow box souvenirs, which was so sweet.

I was impressed with the way the stars were always "on" and prepared. Bette knew everyone's name on the whole set, down to the person putting the spike marks down on the stage. She was unflappable; nothing was going to trip her up. All three stars were there to work hard, and were joyous about being back for more *Hocus Pocus*.

Red Barn BBQ Ribs

～ 2 TO 3 SERVINGS ～

1 rack of ribs

1 sweet onion, quartered

15 garlic cloves

1 teaspoon chili powder

1 teaspoon onion powder

1 teaspoon garlic powder

¼ cup salt

¼ cup black pepper

BBQ sauce (see the next recipe for the best BBQ sauce)

1. Start by cutting the rack of ribs in half and placing them alongside the onion and garlic cloves in a large stockpot. Fill the pot three-quarters full of water and bring to a rolling boil. Reduce the heat and simmer, covered, for 1 hour.

2. Mix together the chili powder, onion powder, garlic powder, salt, and pepper in a small bowl and set aside.

3. Preheat the oven to 225°F.

4. Take two large sheets of tinfoil and lay them side by side on the counter and coat them with a generous layer of your BBQ sauce. Place each half of the rack on its own sheet of tinfoil and rub your dry seasoning mixture into every nook and cranny. Fold the tinfoil down over the ribs and seal the edges, creating two pouches. Place on a tray and bake for 2 hours.

5. Carefully open the tinfoil pouches and place back in the oven on broil for 5 minutes.

6. Slather in sauce and watch 'em fall off the bone!

Grandpa's Famous Red Barn BBQ Sauce

∽ JUST OVER 1 QUART ∾

4 cups Hunt's ketchup (Grandpa was a label whore about only one thing: ketchup!)

⅓ cup Worcestershire sauce

¼ cup molasses

2 tablespoons garlic salt

2 tablespoons black pepper

For a spicy kick, 1 tablespoon cayenne pepper

Pour the ketchup, Worcestershire sauce, molasses, garlic salt, and pepper into a large bowl and mix well with an immersion blender, if you have one. Refrigerate for at least 1 hour.

NEVER GIVE UP

I had my own little Easter miracle this year; I decided to go to my family's Easter party, and was not exactly looking forward to it because I was accustomed to what it had always felt like growing up. And to be honest, some of the day did still feel that way. But then something happened:

I'd mentioned that I was working on this book and that it would include family recipes, and then several of my family members handed me their recipes for inclusion. Including the one we all thought was lost forever: my grandpa's barbecue sauce.

When Grandpa died, it was quick, and he didn't have any time to get his affairs in order—including things like finally revealing his secret recipe. We'd tried different variations to figure out how he made his barbecue sauce, but no one could get it just right. And then my uncle Rooster remembered that he had it written down from when he ran the second location of their restaurant.

He tried it out at home first to make sure it was right—it was—and then he wrote down the recipe for me. For you. It was emotional; it was symbolic. It felt good to have my family's help to recapture something magical. And it reminded me that there is always hope to find something you've missed.

It hit home for me on both of those movies that the biggest stars usually have staying power for a reason: They're the ones who don't "phone it in." They keep getting work because people like working with them. They're reliable, they don't expect other people to go fetch them drinks, and they care about doing a good job.

Even in a more "normal" job, the same principles apply: When you show up with a good attitude, ready to work, and you treat everyone with respect, and you take the time to prepare whatever needs to be done ahead of time, and you don't have a foot out the door the minute your job is over, you build your reputation. And your reputation is everything.

You never know where anything will lead in life, and when the coworker you told to go sit on a porcupine is going to get a promotion and become your boss. Or when the person you were kind to when everyone else was being awful is going to be in a position to recommend you.

People complain that so much of life is about "who you know," but that doesn't have to be a negative—you can know people, too. The more you're open to meeting people, helping them, listening to them, opening up to them, the more you, too, will *know somebody who knows somebody.*

When I pictured my future, you know what I never saw in it? A book deal. But at a conference one day, I happened to start chatting outside with someone who would eventually become my publicist, and she's the one who said to me, "I think you need to write a book." Her vision expanded my vision. I think life is supposed to work that way.

When I look back now on my younger self, there's so much I wish I could say to reassure that kid. Mostly, what I want to say is:

Your path is going to look different from what you pictured, but your dreams are going to come true.

Success to me means finding peace and happiness, in whatever form that takes for you. It doesn't have to mean being on TV—we all have different ideas of what our ideal life looks like. But whatever it is, make sure it's *your* ideal life and not your parents', your teachers', or anyone else's. Don't try to mimic anyone else's route, or you'll always be looking for the next step: "I'll be happy if only I accomplish this next thing. . . ."

But success isn't just about job titles, money, or fame. It's about living your values and having enough so that you can do the things you want to do. Maybe it's about having an impact on others. I've often thought, "If I died tomorrow, would I be okay with the impact I've had?" and the answer is yes—I know that I've helped people to see that they were allowed to feel good about themselves even if they didn't fit society's traditional beauty standards, or even if they were queer or nonbinary or useless at sports or dyslexic or . . . any of the other things that have made me "different." I want to be a role model for anyone who doesn't fit the mold, so people can realize that they don't have to succeed despite the things that make them different . . . the things that make us different can be the keys to our success.

Nobody's life follows a perfectly linear path either. Expect detours and recalculations. If Dorothy had just clicked her heels together three times right when she got the slippers, she would have gone home like she wanted—but she would have missed the whole journey.

The journey through Oz was scary and long, and sometimes it looked like she might never find her way back out, and sometimes she hallucinated on poppies, and sometimes she got sky-stalked by a green-skinned bitch on a kitchen accessory, but Dorothy had to walk this whole long path in order to appreciate what she had and help her to see her life more clearly. She met all these people along the way who helped her and gave her new insights, and she even learned that if you join in on a murder-for-hire plot the great and powerful floating head who commissions you might be a scammer. And that you should get into a hot-air balloon with him anyway. Especially if you're a cute young runaway girl with no worldly knowledge and he's a creepy old guy calling himself a wizard and a professor and there will be no means of escape.

Thumbs up!

But listen, because this is the most important thing I can share with you, even more important than Aunt Glenda Faye's Cherry Cobbler, which is fucking delicious: If you are on one of those detours right now, or that bitch on a broomstick is chasing you around while you're just trying to live your best life, hang in there.

I had so many moments when I thought I was never going to find peace and happiness. I wasted a lot of time thinking I was ugly and unlovable and something was wrong with me. A lot of us queens did. When you start truly accepting yourself, all that fades away and the echoes of the people who've laughed at you or made you feel small get quieter. You have to be your own best friend. Then you can clear out all the bullshit in your life and make way for the bright, joyful path you're supposed to be on and the blessings that are supposed to be yours.

Nothing is ever as bad as it seems. The problems that seem insurmountable now may not even register as a minor thought in five years. So when you get stuck on something, try to fast-forward in your mind to five years from now: "Will this matter? Can I move past this?" Picture your future happiness and think about how you can move in that direction.

Make sure you take the time to toast to yourself—celebrate your successes and the things you've overcome. Celebrate who you are today, how far you've come, how hard you've worked, no matter whether or not you've hit any of your ultimate goals.

Celebrate yourself every chance you get. Be wildly queer and unique. Learn what it means to really love yourself—not just the parts that people praise, but all of who you are. 'Cause Ginger loves you. And don't you forget it.

Acknowledgments

To Paul, Kathleen, Lily, and Jack, thanks for allowing us into your gorgeous home to shoot the incredible photos in this book. Thanks even more for puppy kisses and the best wine ever!

To Mark and the team at Trident, thanks for turning my dream into a reality!

To Michelle and the team at Atria, thank you for believing in me and the power of my story! The care you put into everything is truly a gift!

To RuPaul and everyone at WOW, thanks for giving me a global platform and helping me introduce myself to the world! I'm very proud to be a part of that Legacy.

To David, Jacob, Ryan, and everyone at PEG, thanks for the never-ending love and support you all give me! No matter what off-the-wall ideas I come up with, you help me nurture them into fruition. It's so rare but so nice to have a management team that really cares!

To my family, thanks for the crazy stories, the fact-checking, and the recipes!

To Tina Turner, thanks for inspiring me and giving me strength every single day. Your story really helped me, so hopefully mine can now do the same!

To Mom, Stacie, Trent, Bray, Roxie, and Diogi, thanks for sharing the laughter, the joy, the tears, the meals, and the endless nights of digging through scrapbooks and photo albums! Our house wouldn't be a home without all of you in it!

To Gidget, Michael, and Chad, you're more than friends, more than family, you're my "framily" and you always come through for me. Shooting all those looks and recipes in two days should have been a disaster, but you made it all an incredible weekend filled with laughter, love, and way too much food! "OH NOOOO!"

To Mandi, thank you for believing in me and this book before anyone else! The early morning emails, late night gab fests, meeting after meeting, and occasional smoke breaks in a blizzard have led to this . . . and you saw it before anyone else!

To Jenna, thank you for the more than one hundred hours of therapy! Seriously, reliving my entire life in Technicolor detail was one of the hardest things I've ever had to do, but you made me feel safe and helped me make sense of it all. At this point you know me better than I know myself!

To my husband, CeeJay, thank you for your patience and unending support through all of this. You make me feel beautiful and loved even when my hair is messy, my breath is bad, I've only got one eyebrow, or I'm at my lowest. That's the kind of love I hope everyone else experiences at least once in their life. How lucky for me that I get to experience it every day!

To my granny, thank you for feeding me when I was hungry, making me laugh when I was sad, setting me back on course when I started to drift, and protecting me when I couldn't protect myself. You were an incredible, strong woman and I'm so proud to share your story with the world. You were always the real superstar!

To all the fans, thank you for loving me. Thank you for supporting me. Thank you for caring about what I have to say. Thank you for being the best folx out there. I love you back!

Index